The 2 Shes

The 2 Shes

ONE GAVE ME LIFE. . .
OTHER BECAME MY LIFE

ABHINAV KAUSHIK

Srishti
PUBLISHERS & DISTRIBUTORS

Srishti Publishers & Distributors
Registered Office: N-16, C.R. Park
New Delhi – 110 019
Corporate Office: 212A, Peacock Lane
Shahpur Jat, New Delhi – 110 049
editorial@srishtipublishers.com

First published by Notion Press in 2015

Revised version, 2018
First published by
Srishti Publishers & Distributors in 2018

10 9 8 7 6 5 4 3 2

This is a work of fiction. The characters, places, organisations and events described in this book are either a work of the author's imagination or have been used fictitiously. Any resemblance to people, living or dead, places, events, communities or organisations is purely coincidental.

Printed and bound in India

To my wonderful family.
And a tribute to my late father-in-law,
who unfortunately passed away just two
months before my wedding.

Emotions are the only language that the Universe understands. Be cautious about what you are communicating!

Acknowledgements

'Writer' – a word that flashes the image of a person sheltered in a solitary corner of his home with a meditative gaze at the laptop screen, as his fingers make involuntary movements on the keyboard, churning out an astonishing combination of words to divulge his feelings or emotions! But, it cannot be stated as a one-man job, for even the thoughts and events running inside this magical box are either directly or indirectly influenced by people who surround us. I would like to take this opportunity to thank all of them.

My family: My foremost thanks goes to my Mom, Mrs Rekha Sharma, who is my friend, my motivation, and the reason behind my life. My second token of gratitude goes to my Dad, Mr A.K. Sharma, who is my mentor and my troubleshooter in all the ups and downs of my life. Special thanks to my wife Priyanka, who is bearing the ordeal of living with a writer. Thank you for loving me so much, despite all my weaknesses. I would like to thank my brothers, Gaurav and Prashant, who were always of great support to me; my brother-in-law, Roshan and his lovely wife, Puja, who is also my best friend. They have all played indispensable roles in making this journey possible.

A big thank you goes to my multi-talented editor, Manjusha, who has worked hard to make this a masterpiece. You are phenomenal. Thank you for vetting this book fastidiously like no one else could have! Then come my close friends, Anshul, Lohit, Rahul, Gaurav, Anamika, Rajat, Savitha and Prabhat, who have always encouraged me on this journey.

My gratitude goes to my alma maters; my institutes which polished me at every stage of life to make me a better person. I am also grateful to my mentor, Valerie Holmes, Faculty of London School of Journalism. It couldn't have been possible without your wonderful mentorship!

A hearty thank you to the faculty members and alumni of my universities, BHU (Banaras Hindu University) and Gurukula Kangri!

Last but not the least, I would like to show my gratitude to Rhonda Byrne, whose books have changed my life.

Now get ready to dive into a wonderful and mesmerizing tale of love, sacrifice and faith.

Prologue

He took her closer to the mirror and embraced her from behind, to see her smile. Planting a soft kiss on her left cheek, he rested his palm on the baby bump, to make her feel the warmth of his love. He said staring at her, "I am sure, Rekha, it's a girl! Our first baby. I am so excited. Just in a few months' time, I will be blessed with a precious daughter, beautiful and gorgeous, just like you."

"I will be happy with whatever god blesses us with, honey. But I have a feeling it's a baby boy."

"Okay. Let's not fight about that now. Let time answer that question. I am happy that we are going to be proud parents soon!" he said, planting a soft kiss on her right cheek this time.

A few months later...

"Push, Rekha, push! We want this baby, Rekha. I want you to survive. Don't lose hope! You will do it, jaan. Believe me!" Mr Sharma kept speaking to his wife, while tears rolled down his cheeks.

"Mr Sharma, she is unconscious now," the doctor said.

Mr Sharma clutched her fingers and tightened his grip. "Honey, wake up! You need to survive. We want this baby, honey! I want you! Wake up, I cannot afford to lose you, honey. You are so close to delivering this baby. Don't give up now. We have waited for this moment. Don't go! I want you. Look into my eyes, Rekha, I want you... I want you..." he kept speaking and weeping at the same time.

"Yes! I will try till my last breath," her eyelids opened abruptly and she said with her quivering lips, dehydrated due to the pain. She balled her hands into fists and looked into his eyes. She gave her best, and did what the doctors assumed to be impossible a few minutes ago.

She gave him life.

The doctors heaved a sigh of relief as they handed over a healthy baby boy to Mr Sharma.

The Abandoned Room

When a heart breaks, it doesn't make a sound. No one knows about the breakage. The broken, crushed pieces stick to the bruised heart, leading to intermittent bleeding from the eyes. This happens so often that over time, the bruised heart develops a tendency to look for solitary corners to hide the flow of emotions from the apathetic world. It becomes reluctant to attend social gatherings or make public appearances, fearing that the bruises might become public otherwise.

Scene-1

The Party

23 June 2011

It was a day of celebration for the Sharma family. Sharma Villa was bathed in waves of merriment and ecstasy that evening. It was a moment of pride for them as their elder son Akshay had gotten into one of the most prestigious universities of India, the Banaras Hindu University (BHU). Akshay was usually known by his nickname, Sunny, among his loved ones. He was the much talked about person that evening, and his relatives motivated their children with him as an example. His parents enjoyed the evening, as their relatives kept praising them for putting in selfless effort in giving their kids the best education that they could. But, amidst all this pomp and show, there was someone standing all alone, engrossed in his own world of thoughts. He was unaffected by the surroundings and was immersed in a pool of loneliness. He was Akshay himself.

"Sunny, where are you?" Akshay's mother called out from the kitchen.

Wiping his tears, he said, "Yes Mom. I am coming in a moment." He rushed to the washroom to wash his face.

"Beta, where are you? Everyone is waiting to see their hero!" Sunny's Mom said. She was baking a cake for the guests and her hands were busy mixing the batter.

Sunny walked down the staircase and stood next to his mom, "Yes Mom, you were calling me?"

"Nothing beta. I just want you to attend to your relatives. They are here to see you." She looked up at him lovingly and noticed his wet face. "Hey! Why did you wash your face suddenly? Is everything alright, Sunny?" she asked.

"Yes Mom. Absolutely fine. Something had gone into my right eye and it was watering. But now it's fine," Sunny said, cupping his right eye.

"Okay. Will you serve these refreshments?" she asked, pulling another cake out of the microwave.

"Yes Mom, sure," he responded. He started serving the refreshments to guests, placing a fake smile on his lips and greeting everybody with love and respect, as he was instructed to. The passage he walked through from the kitchen to the living room passed the door of a small room, which was now an abandoned storeroom. He noticed that his steps slowed down whenever he crossed the room. Every time he walked past the door, his heartbeat rose drastically. It was after two long years that he was visiting home.

"Sunny, we are so proud of you, beta. You are lucky, Rekha, to have such talented sons! One landed in IIT to pursue his Master's and the other is going to join BHU. It seems that the purpose of your life is fulfilled now."

"An outcome of your blessings, kaki," Rekha said modestly to her aunt-in-law. Sunny's mother was a sweet, beautiful and a kind-hearted woman and people admired her a lot. Her relatives believed that she was a virtuous soul in human flesh. She was known for her caring nature and generosity. Overwhelmed with emotions, Sunny glanced at her. He went back to the time when his mother would make him and his younger brother cover five kilometres through rough and jagged terrains in the scorching sun. The three of them would pedal hard on old rusty bicycles, and neither of her sons felt bereft of the luxuries of life. They were satisfied with whatever their parents had provided them with. Both of them wanted to go to a professional school to learn swimming, as other privileged kids of their age group did, and their parents worked hard to give them that. It was this indomitable faith that was personified in the boys that nothing in the world was impossible. She had raised them with will power, telling them that if they wanted to achieve something, they should just chase it and get it. When they cycled for long, she would motivate them saying, "Sons, don't quit! Rest if you must, but only to come back with more strength, dedication and energy. Never even think of quitting."

She never scolded her sons for forgetting to do their homework or scoring lesser marks like other parents did.

Instead, she made them realize the importance of hard work. Her way of raising her kids was different from that of other parents. She ensured that she did not impose her thoughts and ideologies on them. They understood and learned the hard facts of life. People seldom knew that this lady, who was now the coveted kitty member of her colony, had to struggle to sell two packets of tea a day. She had chosen to work part-time to meet the growing needs of her sons' upbringing, and to give them the best she could. Her husband, who always advocated moral values and ethics above anything, held a good position in a well-known government firm. Sunny came back from his memories when his father's voice hit his ears.

"Ohho! So, I get no credit here?" Sunny's father intervened.

"No *bhaisaab*. Your contribution cannot be overlooked. You were the sole torchbearer for them," Sunny's aunt replied.

"No, I was just their non-paid caretaker," Sunny's father laughed loud.

The room filled with laughter again and one of the guests said, "Mr Sharma, you are just too much. But the way you have taken care of your children, you should have been their mother."

Sunny's father was jovial. He was fair skinned and had a French beard, and a muscular build of six feet. His husky voice added gravity to his words. His invincible aura and indomitable body language exuded a lot of confidence. He was an extravagantly caring father. In Sunny's childhood days, he would come back early from office and roam on the streets of Meerut with him on his shoulders, humming a song along.

"May my darling son, keep smiling forever,
May my darling son, keep singing forever."

For Sunny, his father's shoulders were the most secure place in the whole wide universe. He would giggle, laugh and dance to this song, waving his hands in the air, showing unwavering faith in his father.

The celebration ended after sometime and family resumed their routine. Everyone went to bed, but Sunny couldn't sleep that night. He kept tossing in bed and scary dreams kept haunting him. He was uneasy and sprang out of bed a little later. His steps moved towards the door that held memories of his past. He moved to his Mom's room and pushed the door slightly open, just to check if she was sleeping or not. He was awestruck at the innocence that she radiated even in her sleep. He cursed himself for giving her so much pain. He moved quietly towards the abandoned room, not making any noise. He reached the room that once gave shelter to his love for six long months.

Scene-2

Trauma

You get hurt, you feel the pain... But if your heart gets hurt, you feel like dying.

February 2009

Standing behind the door of his room, leaning his head against the wall, Sunny spoke to himself. "Oh god! Why did you do this to me? Please save my family, god. Please save my love."

Tears rolled down his cheeks. He tried hard to stop them, but in vain. He felt the lump in his throat choking his breath. Waves of fear knotted his stomach and he felt a sudden numbness in his legs.

"Om shanti... Om shanti..." he chanted, and whispered to himself, "Calm down Sunny. Everything is going to be fine."

"Sunny! Where are you?" his Mom yelled.

Wiping his tears, he replied "Yes, Mom...coming." Standing in the kitchen, he was talking to his mother. She was busy washing up, and was in the worst of moods that day. The silence broke with a question that shook Sunny tremendously from within. "Have you been physically intimate with Neha?"

"No Mom. What are you saying? I assure you that it has never happened between us and please stop thinking of all that crap," Sunny sobbed.

She was breathing heavily. But in his emotional turbulence, he couldn't sense that it was the initiation of a depression attack. "Then everything is going to be just fine, Sunny. I will make everything fine. Thank god, it did not go up to that extent. The situation can be controlled. You can control your emotions and bear the pain of separation! Our family... Our family will re-unite and," she swallowed a lump and added, "good times will come again, beta. I'll make everything fine, I assure you! She will never disturb our family again!" She kept shivering as she spoke to Sunny. She repeated the same lines over and over again, just like a patient with a mental illness. The pain of losing one's son can disturb anyone's mental balance. But, had she really lost her son, or was it just an apprehension?

"Yes Mom. Everything will be fine. She will leave our house forever, I assure you. But please, for god's sake, calm down. Take care of your health. I am really worried about your health," he said with a tinge of pain in his voice. He made her lie down in her room and moved to his bedroom, slamming the door shut.

After a few minutes, his father said, "Sunny, Neha... Come here fast," his tone terrified all of them.

"What happened Papa?" Sunny yelled.

"Come fast beta, and help your Mom," he yelled. Sunny ran towards the living room immediately and was stunned.

"Oh shit! Depression fit again!"

His loving mother was dying mentally every day. He had no option but to watch this happen in front of his eyes. She was crying and kept repeating the same sentences just to express her pain. Her eyes that were full of love and happiness earlier were now filled with fear and anger. Her body, which Sunny used to hug often to feel the warmth of her tender love, was now shivering with tremors and depression. Her palms, which he used to clutch to get her soft motherly touch, were now flailing in the air in the extremity of depression.

"I have destroyed my son's life. I will never be able to forgive myself. Why did I let that girl stay in my house?"

"Mom, look at me please. Open your eyes and look at me," Sunny cupped her face and drew her face up. "I am alright, Mom, and I have no grief. I am perfectly fine and happy. Please don't think you are responsible for my sorrow. She will go away forever, I promise that. Please understand, Mom. Just a few days and we'll get our old days back. I don't like her, either, Mom. I don't love her. I am just trying to stay peaceful while she is here," he said, struggling to pacify his mother. Neha listened to all this, standing like a statue. Tears poured from her eyes silently.

"Yes Aunty, I will go," Neha said from behind him. "I will walk out of everyone's life. I know I am the root cause of all problems!" she said, weeping.

"Please Neha, go! I beg you, please!" Sunny said. She ran to her room. It's hard to imagine the dilemma of a person trampled in an emotional war between his mother and his beloved.

Scene-3

Departure Day / Valentine's Day

Uncertainty is like a dark tunnel, where fear lingers behind every move you make.

Sunny unlocked the room quietly. It was empty, but the events from two years ago played before his eyes like a movie.

For the whole world it was Valentine's Day. But for Sunny and Neha, it was Departure Day. In the morning, when the clock struck four, he walked silently to her room, putting his life at stake. That day, his love was going away from him. He did not know if he would see her again. All that would remain were their memories. He moved to the door, and pushed it slightly, his heart beating fast. He held the door firmly with his hand, as his breath choked even at the thought of his mother getting to know what he was doing. He closed the door behind him slowly. As he entered the room, his gaze was fixed on his beloved, who slept innocently. She looked like a child. Her hair covered half her left eye and ended at her lips.

"Happy Valentine's Day, my love," he whispered in her ears, kissing her cheek gently. Neha opened her eyes and was stunned, to find him sitting next to her.

"Oh! Is it a dream?" she asked. She touched his cheek and grabbed him firmly, realizing that it was not a dream after all. "Happy Valentine's Day, jaan!" She wished him. They drowned in love and started kissing each other like two lovers emancipated from years of separation. As soon as she regained her senses after a long satiating kiss, she was extremely terrified. "Please go away, Sunny. Go baby, please. If Aunty catches us, she will get depressed again!" she said pushing him back and wiping her tears.

"But, you are leaving today…." Sunny said sadly.

"Yes baby," she burst out crying, pushing her face into the pillow to muffle her cries. Sometimes you can't even cry your heart out, even if it has shattered you completely from within. "Honey, will we meet? Will we be together in this lifetime, ever again?" she asked innocently.

"I promise we will be together. I'll always be there for you. I'll wait till fate makes us meet again. Even if it means waiting till the last breath of my life, I will wait. Please don't cry. It is Valentine's Day, my sweetheart." Sunny did not know on what basis he had made that promise, but it was something that came from the depth of his soul.

"Please forgive me, Sunny. I never meant to hurt Aunty. It was a blunder. I was smitten by momentary anger and…," she said and started crying again.

"Don't worry, honey. Forget everything. I am always with you. Let's make a promise today, we will definitely meet again. Our love, our sacrifice, our faith, our promises, our intimate moments that we spent together and our tears that we shed in longing for each other will not go in vain. We will be together again!" Sunny said and caressed her face.

He was angry with Neha for her having shouted at his mom. But he did not vent his anger out on her. "Baby, please don't cry. Have faith in our love. Leave everything to time. Time is a great healer and it never remains the same. We have really enjoyed beautiful moments of togetherness, sweetie. And now it is time to confront the worst of situations, with the immense power of our true love. It's a test that destiny wants us to take. Believe me, we will pass this test as well. Once we pass this test, we'll be rewarded with love forever!" he said. She raised her head and looked at him with tear-filled eyes.

"Promise me Sunny, that you'll study hard and keep up Aunty's hopes. You need to prove that our love did not make you weak, but rather made you stronger. I have full faith in my Vishwanath Baba. He will make everything fine. You are right, destiny is taking us away from each other just to reward us with our love forever someday!" she said kissing his forehead.

"Yes, my love. I promise, I'll do that. I'll prove the strength of our love, not only to Mom but to the whole world," he cupped her face and wiped her tears. He did not know if he was consoling himself or her. All he knew was that he was making an attempt to give life to their dying love story. The sound of footsteps grabbed their attention and they got scared.

"Oh my god! Oh my god! Sunny, please go!" she stuttered in panic. Sunny's body shivered and his face turned red with fear. What if it was Mom?

"It's Snoopy. Thank goodness. My pets always save me from tough situations," he said.

"Go Sunny. If Aunty finds you with me by any chance, and that too at this odd hour, her condition will definitely worsen. I will never be able to forgive myself."

"Okay, I am going," he sprinted out of her room.

Scene-4

Final Goodbye

Sunny entered that abandoned room and closed the door behind him. He was breathing heavily and checked every detail in the room that was once a lively place. The room had not been cleaned since months. One corner was piled with unused stuff, lying one on top of the other. He visualized every memory they had enjoyed in that room. He hastily removed all the unnecessary stuff from the bed to see the place where she had sat to study. It was the same bed where they had hugged, cuddled and expressed their love for each other. He ran his hand across the bed to feel her presence. He touched every corner till he collapsed on the bed, crying like a child.

"Where are you, Neha?" he sobbed and kept speaking. "Your Sunny is back, your love is back! I kept my promise, Neha! I did not spoil my career. I proved that our love was pious, it did not make me weak. Our love is true. Hug me, I need you now, I need you, I need you Neha," he said. His eyes rested on a small yellow-coloured plastic mirror which she had once used. He jumped out of bed and grabbed it. It was old and covered with dust, but he could still see her smiling in the mirror. Just like old times.

"Hey Sunny, what did you find in me that you fell in love?" Neha asked Sunny when he was embracing her from behind.

"That's a tough one," he replied teasing her. "I like your thick clown like nose, your shabby hair and your...." he said.

"Alright... If I am that bad, then why did you propose to me? And I forgot to mention another thing. I am undergoing hormonal problems too. I may not be able to conceive and give you the happiness of fatherhood. I don't deserve you, Sunny!" Sunny shut her mouth, placing his finger on her lips.

"Neha, never say that to me again. You don't know what you mean to me. You are my life and you are the one who made me smile. You are the one who understands me and I want every moment of my life to be with you. You are my heart and you have to promise me that you'll never say this again. We will get you the best medical treatment. Trust me, you will be perfectly alright one day!" Sunny said getting overwhelmed.

"But Sunny, even then if it doesn't work out, then? I do not want to destroy your life because of my problems."

"There is no scope of my life being destroyed, baby. You are no less than a kid for me. And I do not want another," he smiled to placate her.

Sunny returned to the broken mirror and the foul smell in the room. "Please god, bless us. Tell me. Where is she? How is she? Is she fine without me?" he moaned. He looked about to see more of her belongings. He gazed at a notebook among the pile of rotten pages. He opened it and drowned in the memories again. Suddenly, he saw a visible line on a scrap of paper scribbled in her handwriting. He tried to read the words which landed him down the memory lane. The words read: 'Today is my final goodbye to a beautiful world which could have been mine. I feel like I am going to end my life.'

It shattered him and he recalled what had happened that day.

It was the final day of her stay at their home. Sunny's father called everyone to meet in the living room. He wanted to make sure that Neha would never stay in touch with any of them. A few days had changed everything.

"So Neha, today is your last day here, in this house," he said in an authoritative tone.

"Yes Uncle," she replied in a tone of despair.

"This is a final goodbye, okay? You will never contact any of us in life, especially Sunny. You know what I mean. Otherwise, you will force us to take this matter to your family," Sunny's father announced assertively.

"No Uncle, please forgive me. I will never contact any of you in my life. I'll never even think about any of you. Please don't let my family know about this, otherwise, my life will be ruined!"

In the evening, her brother came over to take Neha away. Six months of training at NIIT and her CAT training at TIME were over. She had to go back home to Bihar. After her training, she was to take computer science lectures at an institute, and she also had to appear for the CAT. Even before completing her MBA and pursuing her dreams, she wanted to support her family, so she planned to join the computer institute. The pressure on one's mind increases multifold when career and love are at stake. Every moment ticked like a time bomb as it brought them closer to permanent separation. It was hard to believe how the Sharma family had prepared themselves to behave in front of Neha's brother and they managed to pull it off successfully. Before he came, everybody was instructed with a list of dos and don'ts. Every moment ripped Sunny's heart apart. A plethora of thoughts were exploding in his mind. He was hurt by what Neha had done to his mom, but he wanted to pacify them as he knew he may never see her again in life. Despite the anger towards her, he wanted to bid her goodbye.

Scene-5

The Pouch

Love is like water. It doesn't matter how huge the obstacles are, it somehow carves its way out.

The day they left, Sunny decided not to come back home until he realized his dream career of landing in a good MBA college. After completing his B.Tech, he went to TIME for a year as faculty for Quantitative Aptitude and was busy preparing for the CAT exam. After his B.Tech degree, his brother Abhimanyu moved to IIT Delhi to do his M.Tech. Sunny was the star of TIME in the third year of engineering and they expected a lot from him. When he finally secured a seat in BHU, he was guilty about not living up to his institute's expectations. But at the same time, he was grateful to god that he managed to get a decent college and his parents were happy. He repented that he couldn't make it to the IIMs. Then, he placated himself by thinking of the place he was about to go to. It was the place that Neha always mentioned in her chats. He saw a ray of hope in what his destiny had given him. Lying on the floor, Sunny recalled the last day when he saw his love departing forever.

The heart-wrenching moment had arrived, with a tide of despair. "Okay Aunty. We are leaving for the bus stand and we will catch the next bus to Delhi," Neha's brother said. Everyone sat in the living room with fake smiles. Sunny was also sitting on a chair, numb and speechless. Deep down in his heart, he knew why Neha was late. He knew that she was crying, making an effort to not let a tear slip out of her eye in the living room before everyone.

"Uncle, Aunty, I am really grateful to both of you for all your support," Neha's brother said. "Sunny, special thanks to you! Neha told me you helped her in her studies."

Sunny's family glanced at him as they knew what kind of support he had been giving Neha. Sunny just nodded, without any expression. He knew that any movement would end up in tears. After a few minutes, Neha entered the living room. Sunny looked at her. He was mesmerized by the sight of her sheer beauty. She did not have any make-up on. It was her simplicity that had made him fall for her. He was obsessed with her simplicity and believed that she looked her best without make-up. He had boosted her confidence in every aspect of her life; be it her looks, her attitude, her wit, or her intelligence. He made her fall in love with her beauty. He made her feel special about many positive things that she was blessed with. He came up with the benefits of not having what she really thought she lacked. He was the hero of her life as he was the first guy who had loved her. He loved her qualities and adored her weaknesses even more. She could never figure out why his words made such a deep impact on her mind. What he said was nothing extraordinary, but it definitely had a magical effect on her. She entered the room with a gloomy face. The bubbly girl looked like a statue today, with no expression at all. She walked to the sofa. She wanted to give Sunny a tight hug before leaving, but they were helpless. Sunny's parents tried to lighten the situation as they could sense it would otherwise make Neha's brother suspicious. "Beta, we are happy that Neha has completed her training," Mr Sharma said. "Sunny, take the car out," he instructed. Sunny's father, despite all the hitches, couldn't stop himself from exhibiting his true nature.

It made Sunny happy as he got a few more minutes to see his love before she left. He sprinted out of his chair and ran to take the car out of the garage. Abhimanyu had gone out for badminton practice. He came home just then. He looked at Neha, and both of them were confused, as they did not know how to react to each other. He was also disturbed with all that had gone on in his family and he felt that Neha was responsible for it. He wanted to close the chapter forever.

"Okay Neha, bye! Take care and best of luck for your future," he said, and Neha nodded. Sunny took the car out and opened the front door, wishing for her to sit with him. But he knew that his mom would never let that happen. As expected, his father accompanied him in the front seat. The three of them – his mother, Neha and her bother in between the two of them –

adjusted themselves at the back. Sunny was not able to see her, though he tried hard, moving his head in all possible directions, for one reason or the other. He had to restrain his movement; he knew that it would be easily noticed by his mother. After a moment, something happened and it strengthened his belief in god even more.

"Hey, I am also coming," Abhi came running out of the house, in haste.

"Abhi, stay at home, somebody should be there. Don't leave the house empty!" Mom commanded.

"Mom, I'll also come, please. Everybody is going," Abhi requested. Sunny was amazed at his behaviour. What had happened suddenly? Why was he behaving like that? Abhi opened the door and asked Neha to shift.

"Abhi, but there is no space here," Neha's brother said. "Uncle, can you come here? I think Neha would be uncomfortable sitting at the back!" he asked. Sunny's father was speechless and turned to his wife, as if seeking permission. Sunny was surprised at his brother's sudden act. Hours ago, he was angry with him for shattering their parents' trust. A day ago, he had scolded him to an extent that he had asked him to leave the house, and now, surprisingly, he seemed to be supporting him.

"Papa, please come. I'll sit on your lap," Abhi said.

Amidst millions of stress hormones dancing inside Sunny's head, a little group of endorphins appeared, lightening his mood. Sunny drove the car and Neha sat right next to him. Both hearts were pounding fast, happy in each other's presence just a few inches away. Sunny knew that his mom would keep full surveillance on him. They were not able to move their heads or make any movement that would be noticed. Every moment took them closer to separation, but they were not allowed to speak even a word. As Sunny drove, his father kept intervening, guiding him to drive safely. Sunny drove numbly. Soon, something happened that broke his numbness. He saw Neha taking a handkerchief out of her bag with something wrapped in it. She meticulously dropped the handkerchief just below her seat. She ensured that Sunny saw it, and then she put her hanky back in her handbag. Sunny was curious to see the packet. The only thought in his mind was how he would pick the handkerchief without his family noticing. He was eager to know what Neha had left him. He slammed the brakes as they reached the destination.

"Beta, you drove very fast, despite my instructions," his father said, opening the door. Sunny did not say a word. As soon as everyone made a move, he pulled out that small pouch. He prudently kept it inside his pocket, escaping everyone's sight. His hands trembled as he tried to unlock the door. How could he muster the strength to open the door that would take his love away?

"Okay, beta. Take care," Sunny's father said waving his hand.

"Okay Uncle and Aunty, thank you so much. Bye!" Neha's brother replied.

"Okay beta, bye," Sunny's mom bid the final goodbye to Neha. Neha kept gazing at Sunny and sadly said, "Okay, bye! Please pardon me for all the mistakes I made," she said moving back. She kept her eyes on Sunny.

Sunny and his family walked to the car, and Mrs Sharma said, "Thank god! Finally, we are done with our responsibility. It is a big headache to keep somebody else's girl with you, in your house."

Everybody moved back to normalcy, but Sunny said nothing. His concentration was on the pouch. He was curious to know what his love had left for him. For everyone, it was a moment of relief. For him, he had just gone through a black tunnel which he was always frightened of. His mind was confused about how to act. He had hands, but he couldn't hold anything. He had legs, but couldn't walk. He had a heart, but it was not beating. He did not know how he would move on. He drove back and got lost in his thoughts while driving. He returned from the reveries only after they reached home. The family went into the house with the hope of rejuvenating their happy family life again. Everybody behaved as if they had come home after watching a movie and Neha was nothing but a character in the movie.

"Hey Sunny, where is my lovely son?" Sunny's father called him.

"I think he has gone to the washroom," his Mom said.

Sunny had run to the washroom to open the pouch. His curiosity was at its peak. He took the pouch out of his pocket and his heart throbbed as he opened it. He found a small piece of folded paper, wrapping a thin chain, hooked to a pendant. He glanced at it with wet eyes, as it was the token of their love. It was a heart-shaped pendant, with the letter 'N' inscribed on it. He cried hard, letting all the pain pour out, and kissed the token of love passionately. His mother's voice shook him and he took the piece of paper out of the pouch. It bore a note in her handwriting:

'I love you jaan, and always will, till the last breath of my life. If you get this token of love, I will believe that Vishwanath Baba is with us. We are one heart honey, so I have given you a piece of my heart in the form of this half-pendant. I am taking the other one with me. It is another half, with the letter 'S'. This is a token of our love, of our separation, and of every moment we spent together. Take care of yourself. I'll wait for you till

my last breath, living in the hope that one day god will reunite us. Please take care of Aunty. She has a golden heart and I am ashamed that one misunderstanding gave her so much pain. I swear I'll never ever make that mistake in my life. I repent for whatever I did. I am sorry. Do not worry about me. I am not going empty-handed. I am taking a bundle of memories, and lots of love from such a beautiful family. The most important thing is that I am taking your heart along.

Love you so much.

Your Life.'

Sunny kissed the pendant. He promised himself, saying, "I am coming Neha. Vishwanath Baba wants us to unite, forever."

The family had undergone a really bad phase in the last two-and-a-half years. But it was not the same earlier. They were the happiest family; Neha had also become a part of it. Sunny's mom and Neha shared a strong bond, just like a mother and daughter. His mother would take Neha's side many times. Neha was found saying every now and then, to Sunny's mother, "*Aunty! I hope I get a mom-in-law just like you.*" But time is not static. It changes pace just when you feel you are happy and shows its cruelest face.

'Gurukula'

Scene-1

Bid Adieu

Life is like a book, where one chapter ends, the other one begins, till you turn the last page.

After a pompous celebration at Sharma Villa, Sunny was supposed to set out for his new journey the next day to realize the promising career that he, his parents and his love had dreamt of. He was ready with his luggage. The thought of meeting a whole bunch of new people excited him. He was happy that his endeavours were finally paying off and he was conceiving this new opportunity as a sign from destiny to resurrect his love life. It sparked a ray of hope to nurture the seed of his buried love, which had remained unattended for the past two years, because Banaras was geographically just a few hours away from Bihar. It was 8:15 p.m. when Sunny boarded the train. His parents had come to see him off.

"Okay beta, we need to leave. The train is about to start," Sunny's father said caressing his forehead and patting his cheek.

"There are five more minutes for the train to start. Let me spend some time with my son. I don't know when he will come to see me. For the first time he is going far away from me. Only a mother will know what separation from her son feels like," his Mom spoke with moist eyes and a heavy heart. She was happy for her son's remarkable achievement, but at the same time she was overwhelmed by motherly emotions. "Beta, please take care and make sure you eat properly every day. I'll not be around to keep reminding you all the time. Give me a report of your diet every day. Don't skip your yoga, however tight your schedule gets."

"Maa! Why are you so emotional? I am not going abroad. I'll visit you during holidays. There is nothing to be worried about. I'll follow each of your instructions. Don't worry!" Sunny smiled, resting his elbow on the window bars.

"Okay, beta. Take care and study well. Do not forget, *veerasya bhogyam vasundhara,*" Sunny's father said his traditional goodbye. It's a Sanskrit quote which was a part of the guidance imparted to his sons since their childhood, which meant 'Success and happiness are cherished only by bravehearts'.

"Okay Rekha, it is getting late now. Let's go," Sunny's father said, nudging her to move away from the train as it was about to start.

"Okay beta. Bye. Take care of yourself. Love you!" She kissed Sunny's hand from outside the window and said, "Beta, stay happy and blessed forever. And please call once you reach."

The train hooted for the last time. She kept glancing at her son, holding his hand. Her eyes were full of love and affection. She was sad that she would be left alone at home again. But it was she who had woven the dream of her sons landing in good universities for higher studies. So, despite the sadness, she was happy. The train started moving and his mom kept stepping along with the train till the point she could keep her pace with it. Sunny waved and said, "Please stop, Mom! You'll fall. Bye, I love you."

He reciprocated by blowing kisses at them. He was happy as he had the liberty to see the most beautiful thing he had, anytime he wanted to. He took out the token of his love from his bag and gazed at it for a while. He held it close to his heart and got lost in thoughts. The gentle breeze played with his hair. He had occupied the side seat. He made himself comfortable. His vision was blurred as he was about to fall asleep, but he suddenly saw a familiar face approaching him. He opened his eyes and shifted to sit up.

"Hi! What a surprise? How are you?" a sweet voice greeted him.

Recognizing her face and making the best effort to hide the pendant, he said, "Ohh hi Ishita! I am fine."

"I hope I haven't disturbed you," she asked formally.

"Oh no! Not at all. I was getting bored. It's good that you joined me, because the journey is going to be twenty-three hours long!" he said. They had met for the first time during the MBA counselling. They were from the same town.

"So, how's life?" she asked. It was the second time that they were meeting. She was energetic and excited. Sunny had to make an effort to match her energy levels.

"Going good. What about you?" he asked.

"I am good too," she said. She sat beside him. Sunny folded his legs to make space for her. She happily welcomed it and sat down comfortably. Sunny sensed that her urge to chat endlessly would lead to him sacrificing his nap, but he had to be polite. He listened to her words but kept his mind insulated. Gradually, she began influencing his mood and he was drawn to her chatter. After a few minutes, the unidirectional transmission of words became bidirectional.

"So, Akshay! Yaar it's so formal, I'll call you Sunny. Sexy name it is," she said and winked. Sunny smiled. "You've done B. Tech, right? I'd love to listen your college and ragging experiences, love stories, about farewell parties etcetera etcetera. I have many B. Tech friends, though I am a Commerce graduate. Share your story with me."

"My story? Nothing great yaar," he said reluctantly.

"Come on Sunny, you cannot say no. I know everybody has an interesting story in an engineering college," she said assertively.

"But yaar. I was a student of Gurukula, a boys'engineering college," he replied.

"Are you kidding me? Come up with some other excuse, buddy. If you want, you can escape from telling your love story. But ragging stories you can share. We need to kill time, right?"

"Hey, I am serious! Me and my brother both were a part of it."

"Oh really! Then my curiosity grows multifold. I would love to know how you managed to survive without girls for four long years. Is it the same Gurukula where the movie *Mohabbatein* was shot? You boys also jumped the boundary walls to see girls? I am so excited to hear about it!"

"Okay baba! I will tell you. Patience, please," he said, to placate her excitement because people in the compartment were staring at both of them. Ishita was unaffected by the reaction that people were having to her chatter. But Sunny was embarrassed by it and wanted to keep her talk to the minimum. To stop her from talking, he dived into his past.

Scene-2

Grapevine – A Boon

The environment in the hostel was hot in terms of ragging. We got to listen to strange stories every day. Students who got ragged would laugh at each other to ease their pain. One of the most common traps used by seniors was cajoling the juniors to come to their rooms with the purpose of getting notes. Once the goat got entangled in the net, the game began. They could make the junior do almost anything when he went to their rooms.

There were many cases of ragging that stuck to our memories, but one is really close to my heart. One day, when I went to the canteen with my brother. I saw a huge mob of seniors standing in a circle, roaring, clapping and making sounds. I had never intervened, but that day, I don't know what happened to me. I felt this urge to find out what was happening there and who had been trapped. I found a safe corner from where I could see what was happening in the canteen. A few minutes later, I found a face rising and descending in turns behind the seniors. I was standing far away, but I could easily sense the innocence that the face radiated and it was pretty evident he did not know much about ragging. From his expressions, it was clear that he was getting embarrassed in public. Most cases were limited to the college premises and the canteen was never a part of it. I did not know what came over me, but I immediately established a connection with that person and prepared myself to free him from the seniors. I went close to the group and my presence made the seniors lower their voices. I had a good rapport with them by then.

I went to the guy and shook hands with him, pretending to be his friend. He gave a shocking glance in the beginning but comprehended my behaviour later and reciprocated the same. Immediately, he was set free. I took a long walk with him and escorted him back to the hostel to ease his embarrassment. He introduced himself as Rohan while we walked to his hostel. He thanked me for helping him and also narrated his frustration regarding the ragging scenario. From that day on, we became good friends. After that, I arranged for his accommodation in my uncle's private hostel where we were staying.

"Ohh that's so sweet, but how did you escape and why did the seniors give you so much *bhao*?" Ishita said.

"Good question! Actually our surnames had saved us from ragging. We got the idea accidentally when ragging started in college."

One day, the seniors called all the scared rats to the back of the college. It had a jungle within. A wave of fear filled us. What will happen? What will they do to us? Why have they called us there?

"Be ready bro! Today is stamping day," somebody yelled from behind the seniors.

"Stamping day? What does that mean?" one of the scared rats stuttered.

"You'll know about it in some time. In the beginning it looks odd and pinches you hard, but over time, you will be fine with it," he continued scaring all of us.

"Fear is the biggest weakness and don't let it overpower you, my friends. Don't forget, unity is strength and we are safe

until we all are together," I said assertively and everyone looked at me in surprise.

"Bhai, are you a local?" someone asked me in a sarcastic tone. "He is delivering a speech because nobody can touch him and his brother. They are the Sharma brothers. I think they are, no, I am sure they are relatives of our chief proctor Sharma sir!" the same person said. I was about to cut him short. But suddenly, all the juniors around me started muttering in unison.

"Bhai... You can save us. Woohoo!" They were excited and relieved as though they had found a messiah. They did not let me speak. My brother and I were confused. We raised our eyebrows wondering what was happening around us. We were suddenly famous among our batch-mates and seniors, with the title 'Sharma brothers', and we enjoyed the privileges that we were getting out of it. It seldom happens that a misunderstanding leads to a positive result. Usually it breaks relationships or damages reputation. But for the first time in my life, it was helping build new relationships with many juniors and seniors.

Ishita burst out laughing, unfazed at the fact that everybody was gazing at her with angry eyes this time. It was past 2:00 a.m.

"Let everyone sleep and you continue your love-birds chatter somewhere else," a voice came out of the dark.

"Shhhh... Okay, let's sleep now. It's already late," she said. Sunny nodded.

"Okay yaar, thanks a lot. And sorry that I did not let you sleep," she said while I moved down to my own berth.

"The rest of the story will be continued in the morning. Have a good night's sleep!" I replied.

"Good night. Sweet dreams."

A New Beginning

Scene-1

Welcome To Banaras

June 2011

Sunny was having the same nightmare again; it made him shiver and his heart pounded. He tried to scream, but his throat was choked. Suddenly he heard a voice and a loud horn. "Sunny! Sunny! Wake up, Sunny!" He sprang out and found Ishita standing beside him.

"Oh! Where are we?" he asked, rubbing his sleep-filled eyes. He could feel his heart pounding hard and then realized that it was nothing but a nightmare.

"Oh! Mr Kumbhkarna, we are about to reach our destination. Get ready! Finally, our twenty-three-hour long journey is coming to an end," she said, patting Sunny's back.

"Okay. I will get my stuff ready. Are you ready with your luggage?" he asked, making futile efforts to open his eyes. He tried to interpret the fragments of the dream he saw a few minutes ago. Their co-passengers got ready to get off at the last stop, Varanasi Junction. Sunny collected his stuff, and packed them in his bag.

"Hey Ishita, I am ready. Are you?" Sunny asked, tying his shoe laces.

"Yes, I am ready too," she replied. The train slowed down as it approached the station. The board that said Varanasi Jn.' was soon visible. The crowd queued up to get off the train.

"Let's move Ishita," Sunny said. She signalled at him to wait until everyone got off. The compartment was vacant and Sunny was shocked to see six trolley bags fixed at various corners of that bogie.

"Hey! Someone seems to have forgotten their bags. But everyone has moved out now. Whose bags are they?" Sunny asked innocently.

"No Sunny. These are all mine!" she said, picking one of them up. "Now, will you please help me get all of these down?" Sunny's jaw dropped and he took time to come out of the shock.

"Are you serious? Are these yours? Have you lost your mind? Have you come here to settle permanently? I mean, who carries six large trolley bags to the hostel?"

"No no. Different bags are for different stuff. This red one is for edibles, blue one is for clothes..." she kept blabbering, ignoring his frustration. Sunny took a deep breath and prepared himself for the physical torture that Ishita was going to give to him. He knew that there was no point of any argument with a woman. He worked like a coolie to accomplish this back-breaking task of getting the luggage down one by one.

"So, is this the last one?" Sunny asked with a sigh of relief assuming the workout for his muscles had come to an end.

"Yes Sunny. This is the last. Thanks a ton!" she grinned.

"So, I'll call a coolie now to take all this out of the station!" Sunny said, pushing his trolley. They moved ahead as he loaded the trolley with Ishita's luggage. Sunny stopped suddenly and started frisking his own bag. Ishita moved ahead with the coolie, not realizing that Sunny was left behind. She got busy keeping an eye on the luggage, while Sunny was frightened, moving and shaking his bag as he tried to look for something desperately. He realized that his priceless pendant, his token of love was missing. He ran his hand inside the upper most slit of his bag to check if it was there. He was sure he had kept it inside his bag while starting from home in Dehradun.

Checking the uppermost section twice, he was disappointed. He felt as if he had lost his heart; an indispensable part of his life was missing. He assumed that destiny had taken him closer to the nightmare that he had had on the train a few minutes ago. He was shattered from within. He had no clue what to do. He had assumed that BHU would take him closer to Neha, but the very first day in Banaras had given him a big blow.

"Sunny, what do you think of this?" Ishita said, continuing her conversation with the coolie, and waiting for a reply from Sunny, which did not come for a while. She turned around to look for him and realized that he was standing far behind. She found him playing with his bag and venting his frustration.

"Hey Sunny! What happened? Forgot something?" she asked. He did not respond and continued searching. He exhaled and calmed down. He recollected all that had happened a day before and realized that he had slipped the pendant into the pocket of his pants in haste when Ishita made an uninformed arrival at his berth. He ran his hand in both his pockets and found the chain there. He took it out, glanced at it and gave a relieved smile. Suddenly, he realized that somebody was calling him from a distance. He looked up and yelled, "Yeah Ishita! I am coming." He ran fast, clutching the token of his love in his fist.

He realized that he was now free enough to wear it as his neckband. He wanted to keep the chain long enough so that her initial would linger around his heart, giving him a feeling that his heart was close to hers, 24x7. That was why he had replaced the chain with a longer one that made the pendant end at his heart. He was afraid of being caught at home, but he was now a free bird to keep it hanging around his neck, without any fear and without any apprehension. The thought of Neha gave him uncanny enthusiasm. He moved ahead with a ray of hope. His ears reacted to the announcement of the trains going to Bihar. He wished he could run and catch one of those trains, but he controlled himself. He made up his mind to certainly catch one in the near future. He found a couple sitting on the bench, smiling at each other. He imagined himself with her, just like that, in the same way, at that very moment.

She used to tell him a lot about Varanasi and the Kashi Vishwanath Temple, and she expressed her wish of visiting the place with him to pray for their love and marriage. She was a great devotee of Shiva and she had expressed her unwavering faith in him. She always said that Baba would unite both of them, someday. Now, her love was here in the same city, but without her. The magic of Banaras had spilled its effect on his mind. He was flying in the air and was filled with hope. He planted a soft kiss on the pendant, as a note of acknowledgement to the enthusiasm that the pendant had filled him with. He looked around and found that Ishita was nowhere in sight. Suddenly, a familiar voice struck his ear drums.

"Hey bhaiya! Three hundred rupees is too much," Ishita shrieked. Sunny smiled and ran to help her. It was settled at less, but Sunny had to work hard to convince Ishita that no coolie would carry six huge bags for an amount lesser than that. They walked out of the station and started looking for a taxi. He wanted to go separately, thinking about the embarrassment that Ishita's luggage would otherwise bring to him, but she forced him to travel in the same taxi as hers. There was no point arguing with her and he surrendered. Their taxi was literally dancing on the rough and bumpy roads of Banaras. He kept cursing her at every shock that his body faced because of her luggage. They were making him uncomfortable, not to mention the temporary damage it was doing to his sensitive parts. It was a kind of city ride and Ishita was enjoying it, while Sunny was busy adjusting himself and getting frustrated at her commentary on the way. "Wow Sunny, see the vibrancy of this place! It is so lively."

"Bhaiya, where is Vishwanath temple located?" she asked the taxi driver.

"*Paas mein hi hai madam, aap kahein to abhi le chalun.* We can go there right away, if you want," the taxi driver replied.

"Have you lost your mind, bhaiya? Can't you see we have been burdened with this luggage? We will visit it some other time. Drop us at BHU quickly!" Sunny said.

The taxi driver kept mum and took them through the smaller lanes, taking twists and turns, showing to them the different colours of the holy city Banaras. Silence prevailed in the taxi for some time as Ishita felt Sunny was angry with her and the taxi driver, equally.

"Bhaiya! Do we get autos from BHU for the temple easily?" Sunny asked, feeling a special connection with that place from within.

"*Ji sir mil jaat hai asaani se.* It's fairly easy," he said making a turn into a narrow lane. He tried to peep out to feel the air of the pious place that Neha talked about often. The aroma of the place, the huge doors of the temples and the traditional architecture of the temples gave him a feeling that he was strongly connected to the city, though he was visiting it for the first time. The fragrance made him go back to his reveries again.

"Sunny, do you believe in god?" Neha asked, running her hand through Sunny's hair when he was resting his head in her lap.

"Why? What happened?" he asked.

"Nothing. Just asking. Tell me na," she asked with a little more curiosity. He thought it over and said, "Not in particular. But I do believe in a superpower. Whatever one may call it, god or anything else. I believe that there is some supernatural energy that is running this universe and the one that rewards the good, punishes the bad, helps the needy and generates a master plan to bring out the best for everyone."

"Okay. Maybe you do not believe in god, maybe you call him a supernatural energy, but I am a firm believer of Vishwanath Baba," she said, folding her hands in reverence to Baba.

"Baba! So you believe in some baba?" he asked impulsively.

"Arre budhhu! I am talking about Shiv ji, Kashi-Vishwanath Baba in Banaras," she replied patting his head.

"Okay, Shiv ji, the chairman of this universe, right?" he asked.

"He is god. Give some respect, Sunny," she said, giving a light blow to his cheeks.

"Okay baba, sorry. I respect Shiv ji, Bholenath, and I am calling him the chairman because he is the superpower."

"Okay, but no more making fun of god. Okay?"

"Okay, my baby! Bolo Kashi Vishwanath baba ki Jai!" he yelled.

"Neha, what can your baba do? Can he help us get married?" he further asked.

"Yes. My Baba can do anything. I have already asked him to bestow his blessings on us. He has assured me that he'll take care of our wedding."

He smiled. He was taken aback by her innocence and her faith in god. He thanked destiny that he was blessed with such a sweet and a unique girl. "Hey! What are you looking at? I already passed the request to my Baba to call you there. You will see that Baba will take care of all this. One day, you will realize that my Baba can work wonders. Mark my words, you will be visiting Kashi Vishwanath temple soon," she said.

Suddenly a bump on the road brought him back to the present. He felt that Neha's faith in god was working. It was only her faith and prayers that made him land up at BHU. The vibrancy of the city could be gauged by the buzzing streets. It was colourful, flooded with different kinds of people; Babas, Nangas, foreign devotees. The market place was flanked by big sweet shops, and those selling Kulladh lassi, jalebis, samosas, tea and what not.

"Hey! I am very uncomfortable here," Sunny shrieked.

"Sunny, we are just about to reach. Please be patient for some more time. I am sorry for the inconvenience," she replied, holding back one of her bags which was slipping down Sunny's back. Finally, they arrived at BHU. They got off. Sunny jumped off and stretched his muscles. He glanced at the huge gates of BHU and the statue of Pandit Madan Mohan Malviya, while stretching his limbs. He had a feeling of pride and thanked god for giving him a chance to make his dream career come true. He settled the fare and took a rickshaw to reach the BHU Management Hostel. He managed to procure a separate rickshaw for Ishita and adjusted her luggage in it.

"Sunny, did you find the city beautiful? I am so excited to visit the famous temples here, especially Vishwanath temple," she yelled enthusiastically from her rickshaw which was moving just behind Sunny's. Sunny wondered how her chirping could continue despite such a tiring and long journey.

"You know, my ride was so enjoyable that I did not even notice the city. I got many memories of the long taxi journey imprinted on my hips!"

Ishita kept quiet, noticing his mood, and made up her mind to not say a word.

Scene-2

Oblivion

BHU had a beautiful campus, situated in the heart of the pious city of Banaras. Sunny pulled out his camera to capture the scenic beauty of the campus and the non-human inhabitants of the place: the peacocks, other birds and rabbits. Ishita's rickshaw went on to a different lane to reach the girls' hostel and Sunny's proceeded to the boys' hostel.

"Okay Sunny. Bye and take care of yourself. See you in college!" Ishita yelled as her rickshaw took a turn away from Sunny's.

"Okay bye. See you soon. Enjoyed your company!" he mocked caressing his hips. She smiled in response. Soon, he arrived at the hostel and got off, feeling excited about the new beginning. He noticed that most of the boys checking in were the same faces he had seen at the counselling stage, but he was unable to recall their names. His eyes were fixed on the list stuck to the wall that showed room numbers allotted to the students. His room number was 41 and he had to share it with someone called Ashu. He stressed his memory to recollect who Ashu was and could remember the guy. Going by looks and body language, he seemed to be a nice guy and Sunny was keen on sharing his room with him.

"Hey Ashu! So finally we are here. Remember? We met at counselling?" he asked Ashu enthusiastically when he spotted him.

"Hey brother! Yeah, I remember. Welcome bro! And yes, we made it!"

Sunny called home to tell his family about his safe arrival at the hostel. The very first day, students busied themselves getting used to the hostel environment and making new acquaintances. Ashu and Sunny roamed around the campus and enjoyed the scenic beauty of the place, getting familiar with the different departments. For the next two years, they were going to be inseparable room-mates. They ate dinner together and shared stories from their journey with each other. Ashu laughed at the stories that Sunny had shared with Ishita. They hit the beds in their hostel rooms and continued talking about their journey to BHU. By then, they had made out that they woud make good room-mates. Ashu was a nice person. He shared stories about his childhood and told him that he loved to help the poor and needy. His father was a rich man and he saved the pocket money he got from his father. With those savings, he had funded the graduation of a poor boy who was talented and wanted to study further. Sunny learned that Ashu always stood by his friends through thick and thin. Ashu and Sunny grew closer by the day. College life began, and in the initial few days, there were many induction sessions, and getting familiar with the geography of the campus. Sunny wasted no time in becoming a known personality in college, not only among his batch-mates but also among the seniors and faculty members. The reason for his fame was obvious. He was smart, jovial, intelligent and sporting. Above all, he was blessed with a unique laughter, one of its kind, which became his signature later.

The freshers' party was round the corner and everyone was excited about it. Preparations were in the air as the day approached. Students did not leave any stone unturned with betting on the titles of Mr and Miss Fresher. Needless to say, a lot of money was invested in Sunny's name. Many people were confident that Sunny would win the title. Students prepared hard to win the coveted title and all those who supported them were inseparable companions. Somewhere in their subconscious minds, they all knew who would be the star. They knew that however hard they tried, Sunny's invincible aura would make it impossible to beat him. The day arrived, but Sunny was not to be found anywhere. Everybody was concerned. His sudden disappearance from the hostel spread waves of apprehension across the hostel. The one who was most concerned about him was Ashu. He got really tensed as two days had already passed since he had last seen him. At first, he assumed that he must have gone to visit his relatives. But he got worried about him even more when he did not come back even after two days. The hostel geared up, including seniors, to discuss the matter. Ashu was the only point of contact and people believed that he might know his whereabouts. But this time even he was uninformed, which worsened the situation. Sunny was supposed to give a stand-up comedy performance to welcome the guests as Ashu had convinced the seniors to give him a chance to perform.

Finally, it was time for the show to begin. The auditorium was decorated beautifully. The final preparatory touches were being added to the dais. The preparation backstage suddenly came to a halt when the seniors arrived and asked everyone to gather. Everybody knew that the agenda of that eleventh hour meeting was concerning Sunny's absence.

Everybody gathered there, dressed in fancy clothes. Tension prevailed on their faces. "Look, we all know why we have gathered here, right?" one of the seniors, Pawan, asked. The whole batch nodded in affirmation. "We are worried about Akshay. Nobody has seen him since the past two days!"

Ashu stood with his seniors and his expression was gloomy. He had tried every way to contact Sunny, but it had all gone in vain as Sunny's phone was out of reach.

"So, I want your opinion. Shall we halt the freshers' party, giving a random reason, or do something substantial to find him?" Pawan asked.

"I think the party should not be stopped as all the preparations are done. We spent many days for the preparations, so we should not keep our efforts in abeyance now. Finding Sunny will not require the entire batch. A few of us are enough, and the rest can continue with the management here. It is possible that he may have gone to his relative's place or somewhere else, maybe willingly, and we are unnecessarily getting worried here!" Ritesh, one of the juniors who worked hard to win the Mr Fresher title, tried to make the most of this opportunity.

Ashu lost his temper and said, "Hey man! I think you want to misuse this opportunity just to grab the title." The fine lines of fear and apprehensions were easily noticeable on his forehead and his body language suggested aggression. His 6'3" muscular build could intimidate anyone. But he rarely leveraged it. This time, he couldn't control because it was a matter of his best friend. He placed his hand on Pawan's shoulder and said, "We should take immediate action. Stall the party. If something happens to him, we will not be able to answer his parents. I want to clarify this to Ritesh as well that Sunny never goes out anywhere without informing me. Secondly, I called his home today, asking his whereabouts. I masked my identity, saying that I was an old friend from his engineering college, so that his family does not get worried His Mom said that he was in BHU and that they were not able to reach him since the past two days. She asked me to tell her as soon as possible, if I managed to get any information about him." Ashu informed everyone with a tinge of pain in his voice, making Ritesh ashamed of his selfish motives.

"Yes, I think it's time to gear up, because two days have gone by. We took too long to realize that something is wrong with Sunny!" Varun said. The group was divided into two, based on their opinions on the party. One was Ashu's group and the other was led by Ritesh and had a few members.

"Ashu, you are leading that group and I have enough faith in you that you'll definitely find your friend. Ritesh, you can continue with the function, but keep coordinating with Ashu. Be alert every second to help them if at all they need it!" Varun said, speaking like a leader to prepare his team for a mission. Both teams agreed and went about their tasks.

The show started at the stipulated time. Juniors and seniors tried their best to execute the event brilliantly, trying to fill the vacuum created by Sunny's absence. The stage glowed with many events one after another. Meanwhile, Ashu led his team, travelling restlessly across the city on their bikes, to find Sunny. But even after restless endeavours, they did not find a clue of his whereabouts.

"Where have you gone, my brother?" Ashu mourned, standing at the gate of BHU, after a search around the entire city.

"Don't panic, Ashu. We will definitely find him," Varun consoled him. The silence of disappointment prevailed and fumes of despair burned their hopes. Suddenly, Ashu's phone rang. He took it out lethargically, as if exhausted with his efforts. He jumped with joy as the screen showed 'Akshay Calling...'

"Hey everybody! Silence, silence! It is Akshay," he yelled. "Hello? Akshay? Where are you? And how are you? We are all so worried about you. Are you fine?"

"Hello Bhai. I am in a taxi, and I'll be there in just a few minutes. Please take me to the Ceremonial Hall from BHU Gate," he said.

"I am coming. But where were you for the past two days? We were so concerned about you," Ashu asked.

"I'll explain everything later. But please take me to the Ceremonial Hall first," he replied.

"Okay, Bhai. I am already there. Just come as soon as possible," Ashu said showing his concern. "He is coming," he informed the group.

"Oh, thank god. But where was he?" Varun quizzed.

"He said he will tell us later. But first, he wishes to go to the Ceremonial Hall," Ashu replied.

"Okay. Let him come. We will see then," Varun replied. After a few minutes, an auto arrived outside the BHU gate. Ashu and the group saw Sunny alight with a plastered hand.

"Oh my god! Holy shit!" everybody echoed. He settled the fare and gave an enigmatic smile which was hiding many secrets behind it.

"Hey! What happened? And how did this happen?" Ashu asked, shocked.

Varun placed his hand on Sunny's shoulders gently and echoed the same question. "Tell us brother, what happened? Where were you for the last two days? We were so worried, my brother."

"I'll answer everything, my friends. Take me to the Ceremonial Hall first. I have my performance soon!" Sunny said, stumbling towards their bikes and trying to control the pain in his legs.

"Bhai, are you mad? I'll take you to the hospital first. I don't know what happened, but it is definitely not okay for you to perform in such a situation!" Ashu said.

Sunny moved closer and tried to raise his leg to sit on Ashu's bike and Varun jumped to help him. He made Sunny comfortable on the bike. "Bhai, why aren't you saying anything? You should take care of your health first. Ashu is right. You should first go to the hospital!" Varun said, finally balancing him on the bike.

"I am sorry, my friends, but I'll tell you everything later. Please try to understand. This is a commitment I have given to the seniors and I owe it to them to perform today. I already visited the doctor, and that is why I have this plaster on. Now, please take me to the Ceremonial Hall. I'll feel good there and all this pain will vanish in seconds. I am a stage-person yaar, and the stage will automatically infuse energy in me," he requested.

"Okay, as you wish. But promise us you won't worsen your health. Otherwise I'll make you rest in your room," Ashu said and kick-started his bike. Sunny was emotional about the bond he shared with his friends. They reached the Ceremonial Hall where the function was in progress. They called Pawan to inform them about it. Pawan paced his steps to move out of the auditorium. "Hey Akshay! Where were you? And what happened? Oh my god!" Pawan was shocked at the sight. "Did anyone take him to a doctor?" he continued.

"I am fine, sir. I just met with a small accident and I have already visited the doctor. There is nothing to worry about now," Akshay replied.

"Accident? You didn't call anyone! It must have happened two days ago, since the day you went missing. You should have informed us, Akshay!" Pawan said.

"No, sir. I went to my relatives. And it is fine now. Trust me," Akshay stuttered a little and changed the topic immediately. "Sir, let's go inside. Everyone must be waiting, and I want to perform now!"

"Are you serious? You want to perform like this?" Pawan was taken by surprise.

"Yes sir, please don't stop me. I am pretty sure that I want to perform," Akshay requested.

He was a high-spirited man. He knew that human capabilities and emotions were beyond physical boundaries, which he had experienced at different instances in life. His mother had inculcated this confidence in him. He stood in the green room, dressing up and preparing for the show. He remembered the day when just a day before his state-level swimming championship, he had met with a minor accident and injured his arm. Doctors strictly prohibited him from swimming, lest his injury got infected. But who could stop him? Sunny and his mother had dreamt of him being a winner, and he had practiced every morning at four for two hours every day. He looked at his mother, and said, "Mom, you'll see a gold medal tomorrow on your shoulders."

"Rest, beta. My first priority is your health. Moreover, there are a number of competitions that the future has in store for you. Take part some other time."

"Mom, did you obey the doctor when I was inside your womb and your life was at stake?" Sunny asked. His mom was quiet. She understood what he wanted to communicate. "Beta, follow your heart. I won't stop you from doing anything. But remember, you are the most beautiful and precious gift from god. I won't pardon myself for my entire life if anything happens to you!" Her voice trembled and eyes moistened.

"Believe me, Mom. Nothing can happen to me when your blessings are with me," he said, and won the competition. With the same will power, he appeared on stage. All the faculty members and students saw him perform with fervour and he made them laugh their hearts out. He won the title of Mr Fresher, as was expected all along.

TIME Institute

Sunny and Ashu arrived at the hostel and everyone treated Sunny like a star, praising and embracing him. They were excited about his victory, but equally worried about his absence for two days. He could fool anyone, but not Ashu, who desperately waited for the right time to ask him the truth. After a joyous celebration, Ashu went back to their room along with him, and immediately latched the door lock. Sunny looked back with surprise and asked, "What happened, bro? You seem to be in a haste."

"Haste! Me? Okay, yes! I am in a hurry. I want the truth, now! I want every fact out of your mouth. You can make fools out of them, but not me. Where were you for the last two days?" Suddenly, he remembered something and asked, "Hey! Have you made a call to your home? Aunty was very worried about you."

"Yes, my friend. I called her an hour ago. She is fine now. And thanks a lot, my brother, for everything that you have done for me. I really appreciate your concern and care." Sunny hugged his friend with his fractured hand. "I'll tell you everything, but not now. We will talk tomorrow. It is a long story and it's already too late. I think you should rest too."

"No! That's not a problem. Please tell me. I am ready to listen to the whole story, however long it takes. I can be up all night." But, sensing Sunny's pain, he said, "You can rest. You seem to have had two long days, meeting with some accident and then the anxiousness of performing on stage. It all must have sucked the left-over energy out of you."

"No, Ashu. I am alright. Please do not worry about me. Let me speak. I know you care so much for me!" he said. He slipped his hand inside the pocket and took out a red-coloured pouch. "See, this was the reason for my disappearance," he flashed out the chain on which the half heart pendant was hung.

"Hey! What is this?" Ashu asked in curiosity and gazed at the pendant.

"It has the letter 'N' inscribed," he uttered with his eyes wide open. After a moment he realized and asked, "Hey! Is this bhabhi's initial?" Sunny smiled and nodded.

"Ohho! So, this is the reason. Hmm… Tell me the full story. Where did you go? Why did you go and how did you manage? Don't test my patience now. Did you meet bhabhi? Where is she? Did you see her?" he spoke. "Her family did this to you? Please, tell me. Is it something that *they* did? If so, we can report it to the police." Ashu was getting more impatient now, with every passing moment.

"No, no! Relax, bro. I will tell you this story from the very beginning. You'll get all your answers tonight," Sunny assured him.

Scene-1

The First Encounter

August 2008

The story began when I was in the third year of my engineering degree. I had a fantastic life with a loving family until something happened that changed my life. It was the arrival of Neha into my life. I still remember the day when I first met her at TIME Institute in Dehradun. She was a masterpiece made by god. After god was done carving me, he thought of carving someone completely opposite of me, so that I could be complemented well.

"So, here are the four options... tell me who can answer this?" the Quant tutor Mr Gautam asked throwing a glance at all the students.

"It's 550, sir!" a sweet voice pierced my ears, and made everyone turn their heads towards her.

"Oh, great! How did you do that, young lady?" the tutor asked.

"Sir, if we multiply it and apply the formula, we'll get 550," she explained the logic. Everyone was shocked at her reply. I sat on one of the seats in the last row. It had approximately sixty students. I couldn't see her. Frankly speaking, I did not bother to. I could see that everyone was amazed at her reply as she was new to the class. I did not know if it was her first day in class and I was not interested in knowing either. I was least interested in socializing, let alone with girls. Whoever came out as an easy catch for friendship, I would not deny. But, putting effort to make friends was definitely not my cup of tea. I was totally focused on my studies.

"Is there anyone with a second opinion about this answer?" Mr Gautam asked, slowly moving his face towards other students with an enigmatic smile.

"Yes sir," my confident voice broke the silence.

"I knew it. Akshay, I knew you would have a different opinion. Share your views with us," he replied with a smile. I knew that she would get hurt by my answer, but I was indifferent, and smitten by the competitive feeling.

"Sir, the answer is '(d) none of these', as the condition mentioned in the question is wrong, thereby making the equation of parallel lines fail. It's a common mistake, sir, which students commit in a hurry to give the answer." I said with confidence.

"See? Why hasn't anyone else noticed this? And what's your name, young lady? I haven't seen you in this class," he enquired.

"Yes, sir. My name is Neha and I have joined the class today. It is my first day here," she replied in a broken voice, standing up from her chair.

"Okay, good. It is your first day. I appreciate your efforts. It is difficult to ponder on a question when it is your first day in class, and you had the guts to answer the question. But be very careful when dealing with Quants," he said with a sincere look.

"Yes sir, I got it. I will be putting more effort next time and I will be alert as well. Thank you for your guidance, sir!" she said. It was the first time I saw her. She turned around just to see that back bencher who had spoiled her first day at the academy.

Scene-2

Retaliation

Hatred unwittingly carves a place in the space of mind, granting a predominant place to that person or thing in your life.

That day she tried to look back, just to see who had spoiled her first day at the academy. I looked at her once. I did not appreciate her beauty at first sight. She was beautiful, but not Katrina Kaif who could break me out of the world that I was confined in. It was our first encounter, deprived of even a trace of love. The batch at TIME Academy in Dehradun, that Neha and I were a part of, was not the regular batch of MBA aspirants. It was a weekend one. I visited Dehradun during my college holidays and weekends, and that was when I attended classes there, preparing for CAT. Neha underwent training for six months at NIIT Dehradun. Weekend batches were feasible for her preparations. After completion of her training at NIIT, she had to join an institute back in her hometown as a tutor, while continuing to prepare for CAT.

After that incident, I went back to Haridwar for a week, to attend my regular engineering classes. I did not know why, but often, her innocent face popped up in my mind, maybe due to a sense of guilt which I was trying to suppress. One day, something happened that replaced that guilt with a competitive feeling.

My face turned towards her as she arrived. I looked at her for a moment and she ignored me completely.

"So, what do you guys say about this question?" Sir asked a tricky question.

I raised my hand impulsively, which was unusual. I used to be the final consultation authority.

"Yes Akshay. You want to attempt it first?" he asked staring at me with a slightly confused look.

"Yes sir," I replied.

"Sir, it should be (c)24, according to the Remainder Rule," I said giving unusual stress to my words, as if I wanted to get them heard by someone.

"Hmm... Are you sure, Akshay?" he asked..

"Yes sir," I said in a low pitch, doubting his expression.

"Sir, it should be (d) 34. I think he has forgotten to add 10, which is supposed to be added after calculating the remainder!" a voice broke the silence. Everybody turned around to see who had challenged the topper of the class.

"Perfect Neha! Really impressed."

"Thank you, sir. It's a very common mistake which students commit in a hurry to give the answer!" she said and turned to me. That was the first time I noticed her face carefully. I could see her sharp features, her black eyes, a perfect oval-shaped face having wheatish complexion, and her pointed nose was as though it was poking at me, saying, 'Tit for tat'.

The girl, whom I did not deem worth noticing at first sight, had compelled me to think about her all day. She seemed to be an average-looking typical Indian girl. But there was something magical about her. From her dressing sense, and her attitude, anyone could make out that she did not belong to Dehradun. She was too simple in the way she carried herself. She looked like the odd one out in the bunch of hot and chirpy 'Dehraduni girls'.

From then onwards, our competitive exchanges began. The AIMCAT examination was around the corner and we were nervous and excited to gauge each other's performance. The day of the result of our first AIMCAT was the happiest day for me. I had scored 93 percentile. To my surprise, she had just scored 60. All my worry flew away within seconds when I checked the results. I felt foolish to have even thought about competing with her. She was nowhere close to me.

That day, I attended class with pride, and an exhilarated feeling of getting my invincible position back. Somewhere, I had been afraid of losing my reputation. I was dying to see her, to know how lost she must after for having seen the results. Needless to say, we were silent competitors. I wanted to have eye contact with her, as I desperately wanted to show off my victory, but she left early from class that day.

After a few more sessions, I realized that she was trying hard to score better, but she was not that competitive. Sometimes, I felt sad for her, as she tried hard despite her weak background. One of her friends told me that she had finished high school at a nominal school in Bihar. I also realized that she was hard-working but her fundamentals were weak, preventing her from scoring well in the class tests. Many students got their doubts cleared with me, but not Neha.

After one of the sessions, students surrounded me with their doubts as the faculty had left early that day.

"Hey Neha, come! Let's discuss the paper with Sunny. We hardly get a chance to catch him," Sonal, Neha's friend, told her.

"No yaar, I am okay. I don't need anyone." I had felt sad for her just moments ago, but all that sadness vanished immediately because of her haughty attitude.

"Doesn't matter, Sonal. Let her go," I said. Sonal ignored her and came back to discuss the questions with me. "Sunny! I think I need to work hard on Algebra. I am not confident even when I practice it enough. Will you help me with that?"

"Sure, definitely! Anytime for you," I replied.

"Okay, share your number. I will call you if I need your help." We exchanged numbers. The story with Neha proceeded like that for many days. It was nothing but a cold war that kept going between us for many subsequent weeks.

Scene-3

Shock or Surprise?

Life is the most beautiful and adventurous journey. But, you don't know when that journey will leave you in shock or surprise.

Many days passed, and one day, I received a call from my friend, Rohan, whom I had helped during the ragging phase in college. I had even helped him find a room at my uncle's private hostel. He shared a very good relationship with my family and ensured that he visited my parents whenever he came to Dehradun. He was close to my family and treated my parents as his guardians. Our friendship grew with time as we spent a lot of time together, being neighbours in the hostel.

Rohan called me and said, "Hey, I am in Dehradun and want to meet Uncle and Aunty. Let me know what time is convenient for you."

"Okay. Not a problem. It is your home, buddy. Come whenever you feel like coming," I replied.

"Great. In half hour!" Rohan responded, excited.

"Okay, great!" I hung up and yelled to Mom, saying, "Mom! Rohan is coming in half an hour."

"Ohh! Rohan is coming? That is good!" she replied. "Okay, I will make lunch for him. I know he loves rajma chawal." Saying so, Mom left the room.

After about half an hour, the doorbell rang, along with the whistle of the cooker. I sprang out of the sofa and ran towards the door. The screeching sound of my chair broke the silence.

"Hey! Welcome, my friend," I said while rushing towards the gate. As it opened, I froze like a statue.

"Hey Sunny! How are you?" Rohan asked, but there was no movement in my body.

I was completely frozen at the sight. For a few seconds, there was no movement in my eyelids. There was no inhalation or exhalation at that point.

"Hey! Where are you looking at Sunny? I do not understand," he asked again, shaking me a little. My jaw dropped and I felt my brain go blank. I was speechless. Neha stood beside him and I wondered what she was doing with Rohan. I thought destiny had played the biggest prank with me that day. Suddenly, Rohan screamed at me and I got my senses back. "Sunny, what are you looking at? She is my sister, Neha. I told you once, long back. She is in Dehradun for the next six months, so I thought she should meet Uncle and Aunty. That is why I brought her here today."

"Ahh..." I just nodded with a confused look. Mummy came running to welcome Rohan and Neha.

"Namaste Aunty, how are you?" Rohan greeted Mom and touched her feet.

"Rohan, my son! I am fine. What about you? You have come after such a long time. You don't miss your Aunty, beta?" Everyone proceeded inside the house. I was still not able to say anything. "Hey, who is this cute girl?" Mom asked.

"Namaste Aunty," Neha greeted with a contrived smile, but the lines of shock were clearly visible to me on her face.

"Namaste, beta. What's your name?" Mom asked.

"Neha."

"Aunty, she came to Dehradun a few weeks ago. She is attending the best coaching classes for her MBA exam. I wanted her to do it under your and Uncle's guardianship" Rohan said.

"Oh, great beta! Sunny has also joined classes for MBA. Where have you joined, Neha?" Mom asked.

"Okay Mom! I remember, I have to fetch some snacks from the market!" I said.

"Snacks? This is lunch time. Who's asked you to bring snacks? I asked you yesterday to bring snacks. I have to remind you at least thrice when I need you to go to the market to buy anything," Mom said.

"No... I have uhh... one more... my pen... pen refill! I have to bring it, so I will buy some snacks too. Bye!" I sprinted out. I wanted to escape somehow, as I was unable to face Neha. I knew that she would also be feeling the same way.

"Come, make yourself comfortable in the living room. Let's chat for some time, and then eat. I have made rajma chawal for you, Rohan!" Mom said.

"Ohh wow! That's why I say that you are the best aunty in the whole world. I love you!" Rohan said with excitement. I went outside the house to regain my senses.

"My cold war enemy turned out to be Rohan's sister...my best friend's sister! Why didn't I realize that earlier? But how would I have known that? He told me long ago about her, and we hardly met in the last two months. How will I face her now? My whole family will be talking to her as she is the guest this evening. They will be skeptical about my odd behaviour. Oh god! Why have you landed me in such a weird situation?" I mumbled. To prepare myself to face the scene at home with enough confidence, I took a deep breath. After some time, I returned home and my family gathered for lunch. Abhi and Papa also joined us.

"So beta, where are you staying now?" Papa asked Neha.

"Uncle, I am staying in a girl's hostel near TIME Institute," she said, pouring some Rajma into the bowl.

"Is it comfortable for you? Beta, do not hesitate to ask for help if you face any problem in Dehradun. Rohan is like our son. If you have an issue with your accommodation, studies, food or anything else, let us know," Papa said, making her more comfortable.

"Yes Uncle, sure. Rohan bhaiya has told me about you and your family and how good you all have been to him." she replied.

"Sunny, you are also going to TIME, right? Have you met her?" Papa asked, sensing my strange behaviour.

"Ahh... No...Yes... ahh... I think yes," I stammered.

"I will tell you uncle. He is the star of our batch and the thing is, he never talks to mediocre students like me," Neha said sarcastically.

"Oh, that's why bhaiya is behaving so weirdly and not saying anything at all since you joined us. They've already met before, Papa, and it seems there is tough competition between the two," Abhi said and everyone laughed.

"No, no... Nothing like that." I said, but Papa cut me short immediately.

"Sunny, what's this I am hearing? I have heard this on other occasions too. Do not forget, 'vidya dadati vinayam' *(true knowledge imparts humbleness). Make sure that now on, you guide her in her studies. There is no better service than enlightening a person with one's own knowledge. Have you forgotten that I used to teach you and Abhi when you were kids? I should not hear that Neha is facing problems in her studies as long as you are a student at that academy. She is new to our city and she should not face any problems," Papa said and I nodded. I saw a smile making its way on her face. I think this was the*

first time we shared a smile, otherwise all our interactions in the past had been rough ones.

"Yes Bhai, you should take care of her. After all, she is your sister too!" Rohan tried to set up a comfort zone. Everybody nodded.

"Neha, you won't feel lonely here. You have your uncle and aunty and two brothers to take care of you." Mom smiled. Everybody was cheerful, except me. I was confused about how to react. I did not have a relationship with her, but I did not want to be called her brother as well.

Scene-4

As the feelings evolved...

When clouds of ego vanish, the rays of love shine.

That meeting at home broke the ice and the ego between us. It opened an avenue for conversation. The silent competition that existed between us for weeks ended that day. Finally, we came out of our shells and began greeting each other, followed by a little friendly chatter. I don't know why, but there was a drastic behavioural change that was witnessed in both of us after Neha's visit to my place. The reluctance converted to hesitance, the antipathy turned into sympathy and the resignation changed to acceptance.

"Hi Neha! How are you?" I asked as I entered the classroom. There were only a few people in class, as it was about to start in ten minutes.

"Hi Sunny, I am fine. How are uncle and aunty?" she asked, with a smile. I was confused where to sit. Should I be a back bencher as I was, or should I occupy the empty chair beside her?

"They are fine," I said moving towards her without much thought. I sat beside her. "Mom and Dad were asking about you. I told them that you are doing well." I smiled and looked into my notebook to escape an eye contact. The faculty arrived and the lecture began. The tough question sets were on the agenda that day and Sir was firing them at us, one by one.

"See guys, this question appeared in the examination in 2006," Sir said. Everybody caught the pace and bent over their question papers to win the challenge. Suddenly, Neha's fast hand movements grabbed my attention. I peeped into her notebook to see how she was doing. She struggled to find the answer. After a while, she lifted her head and looked at me, seeking to have a confirmation that she was approaching it right. This was a sudden change in her behaviour, as she had surpassed her ego to take help.

"It's 2x rather than x," I murmured and pointed out her mistake. She rectified it and solved it immediately. A beautiful smile spread across her face and I felt happy being the reason for that smile.

I moved back to Haridwar after that week and was busy with college. I had to skip a few weekend classes of TIME because of my Engineering exams. Rohan kept enquiring about Neha's performance in class. I always gave him a positive response. I did not see her for a month. But sometimes, her smiling face would flash in my mind and I would avoid any feeling of inclination towards her, and the reason was obvious. Things moved at an ordinary pace, until I went back to Dehradun after a month, for four consecutive holidays including weekends.

I reached class before time. I was excited as I would be meeting Neha after a month. I thought she would also be happy to see me. But contrary to my belief, she seemed dull. She gave me a cold response, and complemented it with a fake smile which pierced my heart. I did not sit close to her, but chose to sit with the back benchers. Despite this, my eyes and heart were not under my control. My concentration kept deviating towards her. I couldn't understand why my body was reacting this way. She was nothing to me, but a friend's sister. I shouldn't have been feeling bad if she was not that chirpy just for one day. Why was I getting so uncomfortable? Why was I not able to concentrate?

"Hi Neha! How are you? Look a little low? All okay?" I asked her after class got over.

"Yeah, I am alright Sunny," she replied groggily and turned away.

"Hey! But you look so tense." I got a little concerned as I noticed a tear hanging at the corner of her eyelids.

"Nothing, Sunny. Thanks for asking. I am okay," she replied.

"If there is something, you can tell me, Neha. I am like your friend and you are staying alone in this city, away from your family. I will be happy if I can be of help," I consoled her.

"No, I am fine. I am getting late now. I have to go," she replied and moved away. I was restless all day, thinking only about her restricted interactions and trying to find out why. Suddenly, I recalled that I had her friend and my batch-mate Sonal's phone number. I called her without a second thought.

"Hello. Is that Sonal?"

"Oh, Sunny! Hi! What a surprise! What made you call me today?" she asked.

"Nothing, Sonal. I just wanted to ask you about Neha."

"So, this is the matter. Otherwise why would you call me at this odd hour, right?" she teased me. I checked the time. I was so worried about Neha that I did not realize it was not right to call a girl at 1:00 a.m.

"No, Sonal. She's my friend's sister and my parents care a lot about her. They were asking if she was fine and if she had adjusted in the new city. Is everything okay with her, Sonal? She was a little upset in class."

"Yeah, I know. She is a little tensed these days. Her hostel environment is not healthy. She discussed it with me. The boorish boys from DAV College roam around her hostel in the evening, teasing the girls. Neha is suffering a lot because of them. That is why she is upset these days."

"Oh! So, that's the reason. Now I understand. Thanks for letting me know, Sonal."

"No problem. I wish I could do something about it as well, Sunny," she replied.

"Don't worry. I'll take care of it. Thanks for letting me know. Bye and sleep well." I disconnected the call and searched for a contact in my phone book, which I had saved a few years ago, never expecting to need it ever in life. The next day, when I chatted in class with my back-bench fellow-mates, I noticed Neha's delighted mood. She turned towards me and said, "Sunny! Why don't you sit with me?"

My gang gave a teasing look to me, but I moved to the seat beside her, unfazed about their reaction.

"Sorry Sunny, I didn't behave properly yesterday because of some personal problems. I am alright now. Thanks for being concerned about me," she said, making firm eye contact with me, which I reciprocated this time.

"Thanks for what?" I asked.

"Yesterday, you were asking me about my mood. Thanks for your concern. I behaved badly yesterday. Sorry for that as well," she replied.

"Hey! No need for that. No sorry and no thank you in friendship. Okay?" I winked.

"Hehe... I have heard this before, mmm.. that movie Maine Pyar Kiya, *right?" she laughed.*

"Hey! Hi guys!" Sonal joined us in that laughter.

"Hi Sonal," we replied in unison.

"Sunny, how did you do that?" Sonal asked, bending towards me.

"I did? What did I do?" I asked

"As if I don't know anything. I am so innocent, right?" Sonal said sarcastically.

"Hey! What are you both talking about?" Neha asked.

"Ask him, Neha. He is so mysterious. He will tell us the whole story. This man already knows what you are trying to hide. He called me last night to ask why you were so upset."

"Haa... really? And you told him everything?" Neha snapped at Sonal.

"What will a person do when someone says that his parents want to know about your well-being? What I want to know is, that yesterday I told him everything and he said he would take care of the rest. Today you called me to say that those boorish boys apologized for their mistakes and said that they'll never ever repeat it. I don't think it's sheer coincidence, Neha. He must have done something," Sonal said. Neha and Sonal looked at me with plenty of questions in their eyes.

"Hey, ladies! Excuse me. Don't stare at me like that. The point is that the problem had to be solved and that was done," I said, giving a thumbs-up.

"Thanks a lot. But please, avoid messing with such boys, Sunny. They are not good. You should not do that," Neha said.

"Okay, Neha. I will explain how I accomplished this so-called-tough task. In my drop year, I enrolled myself in DAV College, *but I seldom attended classes. During the exams, a student who was next to me by roll number, used to peep into*

my answer sheet and I helped him pass the exams. On the last day of the exam, he called me when he was accompanied with his whole gang of boys.

"He said, 'Bro! You helped me without even knowing who I am. I know students like you who come here just for exams, but I have never seen a humble person like you. You really impressed me with your generosity. Take my number and give me a call when you need my help in any way, and at any point of your life. It is Rana's promise, bro!' I told him the whole story and rest you both know."

"Ohh! So you took his help to deal with this?" Neha asked. "Thanks a lot Sunny and I really appreciate your effort to mitigate my problems. You really are a true friend. But, please, never repeat such things. We do not know what they will demand in return for such favours. Such boys have gangs and they are no less harmful than underworld people."

"Okay baba. I'll not do it again. But you don't worry. I agree that they are not as good as other boys, but they are not as bad either. They have hearts, too. But I will ensure that I don't seek help from them," I promised her.

"But that sounds really cool to me, Rana's promise!" Sonal said laughing and Neha hit her head with a notebook.

"Hmmm... Now the story is getting more interesting," Ashu sprang up in excitement.

"Hehe... It hasn't even begun yet! Till now, we were just good friends. I'd say that a soft corner had certainly developed in our hearts for each other. A feeling of attraction was there, but I did not feel love for her till then."

"Of course! After all, she was your best friend's sister, right?" Ashu gave a sarcastic glance.

"You are teasing me now? I know no one will be able to understand this. I feel guilty sometimes, but then I thought about it a lot. What's wrong in that? To love somebody is not a crime. To make someone's life better is not a crime. Spending your life with a known partner or friend is much better than spending it with a stranger," Sunny replied, his voice getting emotional.

"Wow! Slow claps for the great speech delivered by our guest for the evening, Mr Akshay Sharma!" They burst out laughing.

Scene-5

Sowing the seed of Love

It was Sunday morning, and as part of "Sunday is fun day" philosophy, I was lying in my bed till ten o' clock. Suddenly my phone rang. The mobile screen flashed the words 'Rohan calling'. I answered the call in a semi-sleepy state.

"Hey Rohan!"

"Hey Sunny. I just called to inform you that I am in Dehradun. We are coming to see all of you, me and Neha." I sprang up upon hearing him.

"Okay. Great! Okay, today? With your sister? Sure bro. How long will you take to reach?"

"Half an hour," he said and hung up. I took no time in rushing to the washroom, to brush my teeth and have a quick bath. I couldn't understand how a mere call announcing someone's arrival could make me energetic, despite being in such a drowsy state moments ago. Something was definitely fishy about the situation, but I did not have time to think about it. Everybody gathered in the dining hall for lunch, to relish the sumptuous meal prepared by the wonderful chef of my family, my mom.

"No Aunty, that's okay. I'll have very little." Neha said, stopping mom who was pouring out daal for her.

"Ohho! Why beta? I have made your favourite paneer too. Don't you like that?" Mom asked.

"No Aunty, it's wonderful. But my appetite is not that much," she replied.

"Mom, leave it. You know what girls are like when they are on a dieting spree," I teased her.

"No Sunny ji. Nothing like that. It's better to eat less and stay fit rather than to overeat and grow fat, and then work out every morning to reduce flab."

Everybody laughed because she was pointing at me. For the first time, I realized, that she was not that introvert.

"So, Neha, how are your studies going? Is Sunny helping you?" Papa asked while finishing his meal.

"Yes Uncle. Sunny is very helpful these days," she said, smiling at me.

"Good. Let me know if he doesn't," Papa said in an authoritative tone. "Beta, what about your hostel? Is that fine?"

"That's okay, Uncle," she replied in a low voice.

"This time, you did not respond in the same pitch like you did before. There is something not right then. Don't hesitate, beta. Tell us, we are your guardians here."

"Uncle, there was a problem a few days ago because of the environment there," she replied. The morsel in my hand did not move inside for a few seconds. I was scared that she may share the story of me resolving the issue with the DAV boys for her. I looked at her, trying to stop her from explaining anything in detail, otherwise I would get a good scolding from Mom. "But now it's okay, Uncle," she finished without any explanation.

"Okay? What is okay? How does the environment suddenly become okay? I remember during your last visit here that you were not happy with your hostel. I think I need to look into

this matter and come up with an alternative," Papa said while putting a morsel into his mouth.

"It's fine Uncle. I don't want to trouble anybody in any way," she said.

Papa pondered over it for some time and suddenly looked at Rohan.

"Rohan, do you know Ashutosh bhaiya?"

"Yes Uncle. If I am not wrong, he is your tenant in the back room, right?" he guessed.

"Yes, the same guy. He left two days ago. If Neha feels comfortable, she can shift there, What do you say, Rekha?" Papa turned towards Mom, seeking her approval.

"That's good. I would also have good company all day. What do you say, Rohan?" Mom asked.

"Aunty, I am very thankful to you and Uncle. I have no words for you. I would be happy if my sister stays with you. I was worried when she told me about the hostel's environment and I wanted to talk to you, to ask if you could help me with getting an accomadation arranged. But it's like god has given me more than I had wished for. Thank you so much, Uncle. I am ready to pay any price for it," he said with a satiated smile.

Neha and I exchanged glances, confused. I thought there was some force which was working to bring us closer. First, she turned out to be Rohan's sister, and now, she would be staying at my house. Oh my god! What was happening? A girl whom I did not even know a few days ago would be staying under the same roof.

Family Bonding

Scene-1

A Casual Interaction

Destiny was bringing us closer with every passing day. You get drowned in the process executed by nature, exactly as it wants. I wanted to escape this, but unknowingly, I was drowning. Sometimes, my conscience guided me to stay away from her, just to avoid being engulfed in any emotional bonding. But, my conscience could reach my ears only in her absence. The moment she would fall in my sight, that voice was not audible to me.

It was Sunday morning and we had returned from our weekend badminton match, which was a part of our routine. Abhi and I were having post-match arguments.

"*Ohho... There is no competition here, Abhi! He won two against you, please don't forget that. He is new to the game and he's picking it up fast. Isn't that appreciable? It doesn't matter where we stand right now. What counts is, where we started from and how far have we travelled,*" Papa intervened.

"Okay bhai! Okay! You really played well. Happy now?" he said, fuming at me.

"Ohho! You fight like kids! Take a bath and get ready for breakfast," Mom said. We concentrated on the macaroni that Mom had made for us. "Beta, I have made a plate for Neha as well. Can either of you give it to her? I am going to put the clothes to dry on the terrace."

"Okay Mom, bhai will do that," Abhi yelled and teased me, making weird faces. I was excited to see her. I knocked on her door and adjusted my hair. I was never raised with the habit of making myself presentable all day at home. But the day Neha joined us at home, we were instructed to stay dressed like gentlemen. No shorts, and no sleeveless tees.

"Oh, hi Sunny! Good morning," she said, opening the door. She was in a casual outfit and it was the first time that I was seeing her like that. Her hair was ruffled like a nest. My naughty instinct urged me to tease her by unhooking the bun-stick, but my sensibility stopped me from doing that.

"Hi Neha! Good morning. How was the night? I mean, did you sleep well?" I stuttered a little.

"It's my first day here. A new place for me, so trying to adjust," she nodded with a smile as she spoke, looking cute.

"Mom has made some breakfast for you," I said, giving her the plate.

"Oh wow! Thanks. Please come in. Why you are standing outside? After all, it's your home," she grinned.

"Thank you!"

"I know the room is untidy, but I was studying and so my stuff is just all over the place," she said picking up one of the Quant books.

"No, that's okay! What amazes me is the pile of books lying on your bed, and how you must have managed to sit on it."

"Oh! It is not that tough. There is enough space here. Do sit," she said, making space for me on the bed.

"That's okay, Neha. Eat your breakfast, otherwise it will get cold," I said gazing at her notebooks. She sat on the bed holding the plate in hand.

"That's nothing. I was just trying to solve a problem, the one in our problem exercise," she said, gulping a morsel.

"Oh, really? You have tried a lot, I must say. You are a hard-working girl." I said turning the pages of her notebook and registering the amount of effort she had put into doing all the exercises. Needless to say, she was ambitious, and wanted to excel.

"Please don't see that," she snatched her notebook away. "I know I am not as talented as you are, Sunny. There is a certain subset of people who are gifted by god. They are blessed with inborn caliber and intelligence, just like you," she said and smiled, emphasizing that she meant all those words.

"Hey! Nothing like that. I was just looking at those problems. What matters is how hard you are working rather than how talented you are. A diligent person can beat an intelligent one. After all, it does not matter where we are standing right now. What counts is where we started from and how far have we travelled!" I said, shamelessly spouting Papa's lines.

"Great, Sunny! I really appreciate your thoughts. But it all seems good only in theory. Practically, everybody knows who beats whom. I have never seen you studying Quant and still you top the entire batch," she said giving me a sincere look.

"Sorry Neha, I would disagree with this. See, hard work is an indispensable component to achieve your goals, but that should be backed with the smart approach as well. All you need is to search for the right key in the question. Look, here, the answer must be (d). Am I right?" I asked.

"How do you know that, Sunny? That's the right answer! I have been trying this for the last one hour, but couldn't solve it even then. That's why I say that you are talented and I am not, despite all the hard work I put in," she repeated, still shocked.

"No, Neha. Please understand! Don't go with the conventional methods every time. Try to figure out what is required in the question first. Here, we can check only for options and solve the question based on the rule-out method. The one that satisfies this condition will be the answer and you don't even have to solve that following the complete process. Sometimes, common sense wins over logical mind."

"That's correct. I was playing with the equations, making them more complex. Foolish girl. Thanks a lot, Sunny. You are the best teacher."

"No problem, I am always there for you... I mean, let me know if you get stuck again. Okay Neha, I should take my leave now. Mom must be waiting for me. Eat your breakfast and continue with your studies. We will catch up some other time."

After I came back to the living room, we decided to watch a matinee show on our home theatre. It was a tradition in our family to enjoy a family movie on Sundays. We enjoyed a lot of family movies together, right from Mr India *to* Taare Zameen Par. *Mom was reluctant to watch the movie this time, because she was making a special lunch for us. She marched towards the kitchen to cut vegetables and get spices ready for her dosa-sambhar menu.*

"This weekend is my turn, boys. I already skipped one last week and that too at your mom's request. But this time, I am adamant to watch the movie of my choice," Papa said emphatically, taking the CD out.

"Bhaiya, are you ready to get bored with some torturous old emotional movie?" Abhi asked, with a grimace.

"Yes, I got it. I am sure you both are going to love it," Papa took a CD out of the pile and placed it inside the DVD player. The name was displayed on the screen.

"Saheb? *What movie is that, Papa?" I asked.*

"Beta, just wait and watch. This is going to be your favourite for a lifetime." For the first fifteen minutes, Abhi and I shared torturous glances. Moving ahead, we were totally engrossed. When we reached the climax, there was pin drop silence in the living room as everyone sat motionless, gazing at the television set and sitting like a statue. All of us were teary-eyed.

"It is really emotional and a huge sacrifice by a brother," I said, wiping my tears.

"That's life, my son. History has substantiated it in every phase. The human race makes sacrifices for one's own people, family, society and country," Dad replied.

"Look at him, Dad. He was so passionate about football, that it was his life. And he donated his kidney, putting his life at stake and sacrificed his dream for the sake of his sister's marriage. He could have chosen some other alternative," I said.

"It happens, beta. That's how life is. Ups and downs are a part of it. One has to make compromises with one's dreams, just to fulfill the needs of the family. Family comes first. There is absolutely no point in building castles with your own success, by crushing the dreams and expectations of your loved ones," Dad added.

"It's just a movie, beta. You should not take it to heart. Don't be so deeply engrossed in it. Come, have lunch. You will love it. I also made rice-kheer for you with the South Indian meal," Mom said while arranging the plates.

I thought Mom was a little unattached to the movie. I believed the reason was that she had not watched it right from the beginning. A good and healthy lunch was more on her mind rather than discussing the message of a heart-wrenching movie.

Scene 2

Getting Closer

I still remember the day when Neha and I returned home from AIMCAT together. Our relationship grew closer that day when we shared our dreams, and were attached to each other with a stronger emotional fabric.

"Hey guys! How did your exam go?" I asked the bunch of batch-mates, clustered together for the post-exam discussion.

*"Hey Sunny! We were waiting for you," Sonal said, widening her eyes, which were filled with excitement. "This time, Quant f***ed us completely!" she added and others nodded in agreement. "Neha, why are you so sad? We have all had a heart-breaking exam, except this Quant master."*

"Neha, what's the problem? This time the paper was really very tough. Don't feel sad about it!" I added.

"You are the luckiest girl here, Neha. This Quant master is available twenty-four hours at your service to help you." Sonal winked.

"Please Sonal, stop! Stop it pleeaaseeee," she screamed at the highest pitch and moved away. Everybody was surprised at her reaction.

"What happened to her?" Sonal asked me in embarrassment.

I ran after her. "Neha! What happened? She was just kidding, yaar. What happened to you suddenly?" I asked, making all efforts to stop her, but failing.

"Okay baba! Let's go," I said. She kept marching towards the gate. I kick-started my bike and made her sit behind me. She sat with both her legs on one side. I drove slowly, not to let her get the feeling that I was leveraging the brakes. For the first time, I saw anger in her eyes. I was shocked to see her overreaction to a simple joke. We rode like strangers without saying a single word. We reached home. She got off and ran into the house without saying a word to me. She marched to her room, paying no heed to anything around her and slammed the door shut with a bang. She bolted the door so forcefully that Mom realized we were home.

"How did the exam go, Sunny?" Mom asked, sipping her tea.

"It was fine. But the Quant cut off would be going down this time, Mom. It was really tough," I replied.

"What about Neha's paper?" she questioned.

"I don't know about her, Mom. She looks a little upset. So, I think maybe it wasn't that good," I shrugged.

"Oh! Okay," Mom uttered in a little low tone. Suddenly the cooker whistle broke our conversation. "Let's have lunch. You must be hungry and so must be Neha. She has not eaten anything since morning. She was so worried about this exam," Mom said, pushing her chair back to get up and go to the kitchen.

"Really? I'll call her. She can eat with us. I think it would lighten her mood," I said, looking at Mom and she nodded in agreement.

"Neha! May I come in?" I asked softly, knocking at the door. I heard the creak of her bed, indicating that she had stepped down. She took some time to open the door. Perhaps she was arranging her room.

"Yes Sunny," she asked groggily, as the door opened. Her face was clearly showing the futility of her endeavours. The tears were easily visible and her chirpy glowing face looked gloomy.

"Neha, Mom is calling you for lunch," I said.

"Will you please give me the plate, Sunny? I am tired today. I will eat in my room," she requested.

"Neha, I think you should eat with us today. You will feel better."

"No Sunny, please. I am okay here. I am not even that hungry," she replied.

"But you haven't eaten anything since morning. It cannot go on like this, Neha!" I persuaded her. She did not reply but just made a sad face which I was not able to bear. I loved to see her smiling and chirping.

"Okay. Can we talk for a minute, inside?" I asked.

"Ohh... Okay... Yeah! You can come in," she moved away slightly. I moved inside and grabbed a chair.

"So, what happened? Why are you so upset today? Is it because of Sonal? Leave it, yaar! You can't move forward by sticking your mind to what people say."

"No Sunny, that's not it," she replied, wrinkling her nose. Then, she bent her face down. I could see a tear on her palm.

"Hey... Hey! Neha, what happened? Tell me, yaar. Is everything alright? Are you not well? Fever... Or any other problem?"

Even a not-so-emotional person would melt seeing such a beautiful girl crying. There was a sudden outburst of emotions that led me to clasp her hand. She suddenly looked up, staring at me with her eyes full of tears. "Nothing, Sunny. It is not related to Sonal at all. I feel embarrassed now, that I have hurt her. Actually it is about me, my dreams shattering in front of me. I do not see any hope," she said and let her emotions flow out of her beautiful eyes. The soft touch of her hands acted as a data cable, transferring her emotions. Suddenly, my glance was stuck on her appearance. Her sparkling eyes, her radiating skin and everything on her face looked natural and mesmerizing in the sun's rays that fell through the window. I had never appreciated her beauty like that before. I could imagine how beautiful she looked each morning. Secretly, I wished to have a chance and look at her spellbinding beauty when she would wake up someday, wrapped in her comfortable nightwear and her hair in a messy bun. She kept speaking and sobbing. Only a few of her words hit my ears. Dreams, independence, a small place and something else of that sort. Suddenly, a raw fear shook me out of this frozen state. I thought that a prolonged stare would make her uncomfortable. I took my eyes off her, and started paying heed to every word she said.

"You know what Sunny, I hail from a very small town, Munger, located in Bihar. I come from a very simple family. I am not as smart as you are, and I do not have a high IQ. I studied in a Girl's Hindi Medium School, and I am struggling hard to cope up. I belong to a family where girls are not even allowed to stand in the balcony, so as to avoid being stared at by passers-by. You'll be amazed to know that I have never even talked to a boy in my life other than those in my family. You are the first one that I talk so comfortably to!" she looked at me with moist eyes. "I completed my graduation privately, Sunny, to avoid unnecessary encounters with unwanted men in college. I was not allowed to go to college regularly and complete my education. I came here because my brother cares for me. He wants me to be independent so that I don't have to suffer after marriage. It is not that we are poor or anything. My father is a bank manager, and he is doing

well. But he's cutting costs to save money for my dowry. He was the sole breadwinner for his entire family as my grandfather died at an early age, leaving behind the responsibility of seven brothers and sisters on my father. This burdened him all his life, making him thin and vulnerable to diseases. He is so weak that he cannot even walk properly, Sunny," she said in a low voice.

"MBA is the only opportunity by which I can change my life. I have reached this far only because of my brother's efforts. He fought for me this long, struggled to convince everyone to make me independent. If I let him down, I would never be able to forgive myself, Sunny! Bhaiya is too concerned about me," she added. She sobbed for a while and then continued again, "But looking at my performance in AIMCATs, my confidence is shattered. Despite my efforts, despite toiling hard day and night, I am unable to make it. I am not even confident that I can pass this exam. I have now realized how much good schooling counts in these exams. I have lost hope now!" she cried.

She had won my respect. Expressing her ambitions, fear and thoughts before me wouldn't have been easy to do. Not only her, but Rohan, too, earned my respect. I was amazed to see that a person like Rohan was so emotional and caring about his sister. I held her palm in mine and kept listening to her pain. She drowned me completely in her world. I had never visited her hometown and had never met her family except for Rohan, but I could imagine the circumstances she was talking about. I felt like living the struggle she was facing today. She had let me into her heart.

"Neha, don't worry. You'll definitely make your dreams come true. I assure you. Your dreams are mine now. I promise that you will never let your brother or your father down. I will help you in every way possible to make your dreams come true," I said,

looking deep into her eyes. We kept staring at each other for a few moments and everything around us seemed to have paused. No voice reached our ears for some time, and no distraction made our pupils move. That moment had a mesmerizing effect on both of us.

"Sunny! Where are you?" Mom screamed, shaking us out of that state. I loosened my grip on her palm and began ruffling my hair, pretending that nothing had happened.

Neha was now experiencing the true meaning of a family, love and affection. She started breathing freely in the newfound environment of love and gratitude. The shackles grabbing her soul were now unravelling. She wouldn't have expected that the love of a family which she had always yearned for would be given by a family at such a distant place, that was totally new to her.

One day she was expressing her gratitude towards the affection and care she was getting from my mom.

"Thanks for everything, Sunny! I am thankful to your entire family."

I could see the feeling of being loved lurking deep in her eyes. Love carves out a different spark in your eyes that no tangible or intangible thing can ever buy.

"That's okay, Neha. But suddenly, what happened? Why being so grateful?" I asked.

"Actually, yesterday was a stormy night, if you noticed," she added.

"Yes, I know that. Could you sleep well? I am such an idiot. How could I forget to ask?"

"Yes, I did, all because of aunty. Last night, I was very scared, and was not able to sleep. I was missing my mom terribly, whom I used to hug in such situations."

"Oh, really?"

"Yes. Yesterday, when I was yearning for my mother, someone knocked at the door and I got scared. I heard a voice saying, 'Beta I am here to see whether my child is sleeping properly or not'. It was aunty and then she slept with me. She kept caressing my hair with a motherly touch and I enjoyed a peaceful sleep after a long, long time!" she said. "You are really lucky, Sunny. And the girl, who would step into this family being the daughter-in-law, would be the luckiest." I don't know whether it was a hint, but I could feel that she was very happy.

"Yeah, Mom is like that." I grinned.

I spent that night tossing in bed, fantasizing about new inferences that her words were making. Is that some sort of a hint? Not sure, but she had procured a significant place in everyone's heart too soon and we were sharing a great time together.

Scene-3

The first knock

The relationship between Mom and Neha was getting stronger every day. They began spending a lot of time together, being the only two in the house for most of the day. Neha now had a mom at a home away from her own home. Mom got a companion and a daughter to spend time with. They would help each other and share gossip. Mom was caring, as she wanted to help Neha with her physical and hormonal problems. She made her learn yoga and pranayama, and inculcated in her the habit to practice it every day. Mom bagged a large credit in reshaping her personality. Everyone who had seen Neha months earlier would ask Mom, "Mrs Sharma, what do you give her to eat? She has grown so healthy and is glowing. She has changed drastically in her personality and her confidence."

Neha would blush in response.

"That's great, bro. That means Aunty likes her too much. So, you must not have faced any issue on her part?" Ashu asked, setting his pillow on his seat.

"Issue?" Sunny grimaced sarcastically. "You see only that side of a person that you want to see, Ashu. I have seen Mom taking caring of her and even ignoring the quibbles. But the story took a completely different turn when I started committing mistakes," Sunny added.

I still remember when Rohan paid a visit to our place, to see Neha. Things had started shaping for both of us by then.

In that fun-rich environment, an idea popped up in Abhi's head.

"Sehestradhara! Wow, great fun! Yeah, let's go there today!" Rohan said with excitement.

"Great, we'll have fun together," I added. Neha moved out of the conversation silently and we continued discussing the plan and ways to implement it. After a few minutes, Mom entered the room.

"Hey... Bachhon! My beti will also go," Mom announced in an authoritative tone.

"No problem Aunty. I know Bhaiya will not allow me. He will never let me go anywhere because of my exams," Neha said.

"Who is the older one here, Rohan or me? Who has the authority? That's my order. No one will go out without my darling daughter," Mom commanded at us.

"But Aunty..." Rohan stammered.

"That's my order, Rohan. Or else no one will go," Mom said and slung her arm over Neha's shoulders. She smiled in return and as Mom left the room, she teased everyone with her overstretched smile and a wink. "You guys carry on with discussing the plan and wait for me. I'll take time to get ready," she said with a tone of superiority. We all shared a glance of astonishment, but I admit that I was really happy from inside.

Sehestradhara is a scenic spot that is known for its natural stream of water containing medicinal benefits. Apart from fun-loving visitors, people used to visit that place for their skin treatments as well. For us, it was nothing new; but for Rohan and Neha, it was a super exciting journey as they were visiting it for the first time. Rohan was scared at every step as Neha was unable to trek easily. Abhi and I walked fast through the rough rocky terrains. Neha tried to catch up with us, but she had to try hard to match our steps. We kept stopping in between to fill the gap. "Come fast, Rohan and Neha! We will enjoy the falls up there," I said.

"Bhai, let's enjoy the falls from here. Why climb up?" Rohan asked, and Neha echoed the same. "Yes Sunny, this one is beautiful."

"Ohh, really? But the upper one is the best, I believe!" Abhi teased her and we both laughed loudly.

"Yaar Sunny. Neha will not be able to make it to the top," Rohan said, pushing her up on a huge rock.

"Bhai, you are a weak leader. Let me show you how you should lead!" I said and stepped down. "Neha, he is so lazy. Give me your hand!" I held her hand and began climbing the terrain with her, leaving Rohan in shock. We reached the destination faster than both Rohan and Abhi did together.

"See Bhai, that's called leadership," Neha yelled while waiting for both of them. She was filled with pride, as if she

had won a race. We were lost in the magical breeze that was playing with our hair, and we spread out our arms to feel it. The best part was that our hands were still connected. "This is so beautiful, Sunny. I want to feel this air in my soul," she said breathing deeply.

We waited for a few moments and looked at each other with a smile. I was taking a deep dive in her eyes, and my body was reluctant to move. I wished that moment would freeze forever. We shared something inexplicable through our eyes. The soft touch of her hands sent currents up my body and I wished it would stay with me forever. Her presence made the world seem beautiful to me, and my life was worth spending with a person like her. Absolutely nothing had changed outside; the same family, the same friends, the same home, the same set of acquaintances every day, and the same ambience. But I realized the world inside me was changing, bit by bit. The feeling of togetherness infused tremendous urges in me, to enjoy life. Sudden breathing sounds brought us out of our wonderland, and we released each other's grip immediately.

"Bhaiya, tell me, who reached first?" Abhi asked me with heavy breaths.

"I reached man. I know, I won," Rohan snapped.

"Okay… I'll tell you who won!" Neha said.

"Yes Neha, you tell us, who won? Your decision will be taken as final," Abhi said while gazing at Rohan.

"The winners are Sunny and me! Yippieeee!" she yelled and we burst out laughing. We had a great picnic that day and it was fun, running, playing, laughing together. We burst out into gales of laughter while heading back home. The family gathered for tea. We sat in the living room, sharing the day's experience. We enjoyed the aroma of Mom's special cardamom tea. I knew that

Neha was my friend's sister, but I did not want to suppress my feelings for her now, which were too wonderful. Nowhere did I find anything wrong in that. I placated my mind saying that my feelings were pure and there was nothing wrong in having an emotional connection with anyone. I wanted to keep her happy, see her happy and help her make her dreams become a reality.

"Mom, you know what? Everybody's stamina was tested today, especially Rohan's. Neha climbed the steep cliff faster than Rohan!" Abhi said, munching a samosa.

"Ohh really! Wow, Neha. You are a strong girl," Mom said smiling at her.

"No Aunty, that's because I was not alone," Neha said. "Sunny accompanied me while trekking!" she looked at me with a confident smile for longer than usual. Her smile was not the regular one. It was a smile that carried gratitude, affection and togetherness with it. I reciprocated with a smile that lasted for a few seconds more than hers did. That smile took someone else's smile away.

Mom's expressions underwent a sudden change when she saw both of us smiling at each other. Maybe she sensed something contrary to her wish, in compliance with her fear. "Neha beta, I think you should go and study now," Mom said.

"Okay, Aunty!" she replied and left for her room. Maybe she had sensed what I was still doubtful about. I observed the change in Mom's mood for the rest of the day, which made my blood cold. I couldn't understand the reason for her change in mood. She had never behaved that way before. Was it really because of Neha and me? Or was it something else? I wished it would be the latter, but how could I clarify it? I waited for dinner to sort everything out. I went to the kitchen and tried to break the ice. I tried to peep inside her heart just to sense her emotions.

"Wow Mom, what an aroma! What's cooking?" I asked, grabbing her shoulders from behind.

"So there is something that draws you to your mom!" she taunted, chopping the onions. I sensed the sarcasm lurking behind that sentence. "It's your favourite aloo-gobhi," Mom added after a little pause.

"Oh great! Mom, you are the best. I love it." I grabbed the opportunity to divert her mood and kissed her cheek. I snatched the onion from her hands and started chopping it.

"What are you doing, Sunny?" Mom said while taking the onion back from me.

"No problem Mom. I have come here to help you," I told grabbing the gobhi and started chopping that too.

"Ohho! What happened? Are you trying to entice your Mom? I sense something cooking in your head. Tell me beta, what do you want?"

"No Mom. I always help you. See, I have learnt to cut it so fast. You don't know we cook on our own in our hostel sometimes, when the cook is on leave."

That day, I sensed some smoke emanating out of my home, which was definitely not escaping from the chimneys of our kitchen, but the one that originated from the living room that afternoon. I tried to ignore it.

Scene-4

Embracing her Dream

Neha's dreams were mine now. I made every effort to help and guide her. We worked for hours together on her weak areas. I gave her full liberty to call or text me anytime 24x7, to get any doubt clarified. Neither of us had given a single thought to the consequences. We moved ahead with what our hearts told us was right. We did not realize that the closeness between us could land us in trouble.

"So Neha, I think you are gaining a lot of confidence now. What do you say?" I asked her when I called her from Haridwar.

"Yes, Sunny. Thank you so much. I can't express my gratitude enough," she said.

"Hehe. No need for it, Neha. In friendship, there is no sorry, and no thank you. Remember?" I asked her.

"Right, Sunny. But that's not fair. I never do anything that makes you say thanks to me," she said.

"Forget it, yaar. You are a reason yourself for me to be thankful about, towards destiny," I replied.

"Sunny, you cannot be convinced by any means. Anyway, are you coming this weekend?"

"I am not sure, Neha. I have got a lot of things to do this weekend," I replied.

"Okay. So you cannot finish them from home? Forget it, sorry! I will not ask again," she said. I was glad to see her longing for me. I loved this feeling of being needed by someone, so deeply.

"Don't worry Neha, I'll come, for sure," I told her to make her happy. We were unspoken lovers by then. We did not commit ourselves to each other and we did not speak those three magical words, but we knew that we had entered into some kind of relationship of expectations. The following weekend, I wanted to give more thrust to her studies as I had to boost her confidence for AIMCAT.

I went to Neha's room and knocked at the door, but found that it was already open.

"I kept it open for you. I knew you would come," Neha said with a welcoming smile. She sat like a teddy bear on the bed, with her glasses on. Her pen was stuck between her teeth, looking cuter than ever before. I sat next to her. She was mumbling something under her breath.

"Should I bring you some food?" I teased.

"No thanks, partner. I am good. Let's get back to studies now," she said.

"Okay. I have just come to take notes." I winked.

"Sunny, I wanted to say something to you," she said lowering her tone.

"Tell me, what happened, Neha? There is nothing to ponder so much. You can say those three magical words to me anytime," I mocked.

"Sunny! This is no joke. I am serious," she snapped.

"Okay baba, sorry. Tell me, what happened?" I said.

"Nothing yaar. Let's concentrate on our studies," she said and lifted her book that was lying on the pillow.

"What is this Neha? First you trigger my curiosity and then you change the topic completely. I am not going to stay here. I am going back. Best of luck, Miss Neha!" I said, exasperated.

"Hey Sunny! Sorry yaar. Please sit down. I need you," she requested. I sat back. "Sunny, actually, I am not sure about it. But please don't misunderstand me. I have this intuition that aunty doesn't like our togetherness. Her behaviour has changed towards me slightly," she said slowly, gazing directly into my eyes.

"No Neha. I don't think so. It's just because Mom's mood keeps fluctuating sometimes," I said but I knew that she was right in her judgment.

"Okay Sunny. If you say so. You know her better. Maybe I am wrong," she said, smiling.

"Ohh my god, Sunny! Power cut at such a crucial time. How will I prepare for tomorrow's AIMCAT now?" She was restless.

"Don't worry. When people can have candle light dinners, then why can't we have candle light studies?" I said to placate her. I went to the kitchen to look for candles where I encountered Mom.

"Beta, have you taken your notes? I will give the candle to Neha. You go and study in your room," Mom ordered.

"No, Mom. We have a common notebook, as I have forgotten mine in Haridwar. How will she study then?"

"That means you'll study together again? Alright! But Sunny, please be careful about your studies. I am not against your helping her, but I would not tolerate if it affects your performance," she warned me for the first time.

"Okay, Mom. Don't worry. Have faith. You'll see the results," I appeased her and gave her a smile. I entered Neha's room with a lit candle.

"Tantadaannn.... Here is light, Miss Neha," I said in a jubilant mood.

"Thank god, I was really scared here," she replied.

"Aauuu," I stumbled at the edge of a chair and the candle fell down.

"Ohho... Sunny, be careful. Are you alright?" she asked.

"Yes, I am okay. But with a broken leg," I howled.

"Offoo! Sunny, you are so careless," she said with pain and care in her voice that really touched me.

"Don't worry Neha. I have a matchstick. We can light it again."

I lit the candle again. The light had extinguished darkness, only to make our faces glow. Our countenances glittered in that dim light and our eyes were stuck to each other's. Her emerald like eyes left a hypnotic magical effect. I secretly wished that power would never come back in this lifetime. Just glancing at those eyes was truly blissful. "Ouchhhh."

"What happened now, Sunny? Show me your hand. Oh my god! Leave this candle. I'll place it somewhere safe." She took the candle away from me and made it rest on the table. She grabbed my palm immediately, to see the molten wax. "Is it hurting Sunny? Should I apply something?" she asked.

"Ahhh... It's okay..." I deliberately exaggerated the pain. Maybe I wanted her to shower me with attention. I wanted her to keep holding my hand like that forever.

"Just wait for a while. I have Boroline," she said and impetuously sprang out of bed to fetch that.

"Show me, Sunny. Don't worry. It'll take your pain away," she said and applied the antiseptic cream. It gave a soothing effect to my palm, and to my heart as well. She looked innocent and concerned, and I wished to kiss her cheek.

"Is it fine Sunny? Better?" she asked.

"Hmm... Yes! I am fine now," I stuttered. After some time, Abhi entered the room and it was lit up with another candle.

"Hey! How are your preparations going on?" he asked.

"Fine Abhi. How about yours?" Neha asked.

"I don't study for exams. If I love something, and I feel like learning it, I study. That's it," he replied holding a thick Millman Halkias *of Electronics in his hand.*

"Bhai, what happened to your hand?" he asked me.

"Oh! He burnt his hand with molten wax. So, I applied some Boroline. That's it," Neha replied to him. Abhi burst out laughing. Neha was shocked at his behaviour and I got worried.

"Bhaiya got burnt by wax... haha haha ha ha ...Ohhhooo.... Neha, we used to play with molten wax when we were kids. And bhaiya's skin is completely immune to it."

She looked at me with surprise writ all over her face. I smiled and shrugged, pretending to be innocent.

Scene-5

Propose in Disguise

We went to appear for the AIMCAT together the very next day on my bike. I was trying to make her revise the key points while riding. I felt like I was writing two exams in parallel, and I was more concerned about the second. It was obvious as I couldn't stand to see tears in her eyes. We checked the seating arrangements and one of the coordinators made us part ways, indicating different class rooms. "Bye, Neha. Best of luck! Do well!" I said.

"Thanks Sunny. Same to you," she replied. Her eyes were exuding a sense of gratitude. I don't know what happened to her, but suddenly, she ran towards me.

"What happened? The exam is about to start. You need anything?" I asked her. Her breath was heavy and she did not say even a word. "What happened, Neha? Go and give it your best shot today!" I said holding her hand.

"I'll try my best and will not let you down. I just wanted to say thanks," she said. I felt that she wanted to hug me that moment, but couldn't. We marched to our respective exam-rooms to proceed for our three-hour long battle between the question-paper and our mind. For the first time, the three hours stretched on for so long. With every question I attempted, I kept thinking whether she would be able to solve it or not. I wondered whether I had told her about the tricks to solve them or not. What was happening to me? As the exam got over, I immediately ran out of the exam room, like a prisoner out of jail, to see her. "How did the exam go?" I asked.

"It is the first time that I am feeling a little satisfied after an exam, Sunny," she said optimistically.

"That's great. Thank god. I kept praying for you all the while," I said.

"I know that Sunny, because the hard work was yours. You were more worried about my exam." She grinned. "I don't think it matters to a genius. But for the sake of formality I am asking, how did your exam go?" she asked.

"It was okay, Neha. But this time I am not sure if I will nail it properly or not," I replied.

"You can't say that, Sunny," she said, shocked.

"Yaar, during my exam, I was just thinking about you and wondering if you would solve a question, use this trick or that trick. Don't worry, yaar. I can pick up any time. My primary concern is you right now," I said while looking into her eyes.

"Sunny, I won't continue like this, if it is going to affect your studies. I assumed that you were revising the topics with me, and so it won't affect your results."

"Ohhoo Neha. Fine, it was not that bad. It was average. But not as good as other exams," I placated her.

"Not that bad? I want you to continue securing the topmost rank, Sunny. Otherwise, I'll move away from you. Is that clear?" she said and turned around.

"Neha, please yaar. Don't behave like that and please don't spoil your mood. Let's celebrate today. It is big day for you," I said.

"Celebrate? What for?" she asked.

"This is the first time you feel satisfied with your exam. So let's go to McDonald's and have a small treat," I replied.

"Okay. We don't have time left. Aunty is not in a good mood these days. I don't understand why you don't care. I think

we should let Aunty know that we are just good friends and she should not worry about anything," she said.

"Seriously, Neha? Are we just good friends and nothing of that sort exists between the two of us?" I asked raising my eyebrows.

"Sunny, let's go to McDonald's now," she commanded, ignoring my words completely. Later, I realized my mistake. Because I knew what I had touched was a naked electric wire. We went to McDonald's and sat there for an hour. She discussed the strictness that her family had imposed on her with me, and the conservative society she lived in. She terrorized the situation by reciting a story when her father threw a boy in lockup, just because he was trying to talk to her. "Do you know my father's opinion on love, Sunny? He says that he will cut my legs if I even think about it," she explained with moist eyes.

"Ohh my god! Really? Why is he so strict? You are cultured, well-mannered and still he uses such language?"

"Sunny, he is not a bad person. The struggle and pain he has gone through in his youth has made him that way. He is too strict to be convinced for a love marriage. You know, he worked hard, day and night, for his sister's wedding? He was burdened by a loan. On the day of the wedding, she eloped with her lover. He was shattered by the incident, but is still standing strong. After his father's death in his childhood, he managed to take care of the entire family and got his brothers and sisters married into good families. I can feel his pain and I don't want to make a mistake that could cause him pain," she said with a quivering voice. I just nodded.

That day, I felt pained, because the haunting images of her father not letting my potential love-story blossom kept revolving in my mind. I tried to find a solution, but it was in vain. I wondered whether to accept the fact that I had fallen in love with Neha, or stop myself from slipping into the net, which would otherwise make it even tougher for me to come out later. It took me no time to understand that Mom had sensed what had started taking shape in my mind, even when I was unable to make any clear picture of it myself. A few days later, when I was in Haridwar, I got a call from Neha.

"Hi Sunny, how are you?" she yelled in excitement.

"I am good. But you sound so chirpy. What happened?" I asked.

"Yes! I am very happy, Sunny. You are really awesome!"

"Will you tell me or just keep beating around the bush?" I asked.

"Yes, I am jumping in happiness because I can see my dreams coming true. I have scored 80 percentile this time."

"Oh really? Wow! Great yaar! You deserve this, as you had really worked very hard for it this time," I said.

"No, Sunny, please don't give me credit. I worked hard earlier too, but could never think about making it beyond 60. It's all because of your guidance that this has happened. And I really love you for it," she said, gushing with gratitude.

"Okay baba. I acknowledge your gratitude. Now, you owe me a treat, but wait, before that, I would like to check my results. Hold on, I am online." After few moments I said, "Congratulations Neha! You have beaten me this time, with one percentile." My voice was grave. She knew I was not kidding.

"No Sunny. I can't believe that. Check again," she was shocked. That incident shook us. She felt guilty for keeping me occupied and for having affected my performance. Later that day, Mom drove a nail on my growing relationship with Neha.

"Beta, I can't believe you scored lower than Neha! I warned you earlier that I will not tolerate any compromise on your studies. You know well, Sunny, since your childhood, I have been worried about your studies. I mean it now too. If Neha is obstructing your career, I'll waste no time in sending her back to her hostel. She should also understand the importance of your time. I understand that you help her as a brother, but beta, you have your own goals and targets which must be given priority. At no cost will I let you compromise on them." I just listened patiently. She did not only warn me earlier to stay away from Neha, but also added a security zone by calling me her brother.

Mom was getting possessive of me and it resulted in abhorrence for Neha. Her behaviour towards Neha began changing, and she had a reason to hate her. A mother who had struggled hard all her life to get her son reach this stage was suddenly trapped in the fear of losing her son; a fear that her son would spoil his life and career, a fear that her years of hard work would go waste because of a girl. The source of the fear was the fact that Mom had arranged it. She was the one who brought Neha to Sharma Villa. She was the one who gave so much love to her. She hated love relationships because she had lost her own talented and disciplined brother because of a silly relationship.

"Hello, Mom. What's the plan for this weekend?" I asked when I called her one evening from Haridwar.

"Nothing special, beta. I think you should prepare for your exams now and avoid unnecessary travel. I suggest that you stay in Haridwar and prepare well."

"But Mom, I can study better at home," I tried to convince her.

"No beta, my decision is final."

I understood why Mom had imposed her decision on me. The fear that lingered in her heart had finally taken shape and *she wanted to keep me away. Neha and I were already going through a rough and frustrating phase as we were trying to ignore each other. We sensed that it would lead us to big trouble. Her family was pressurizing her for good results. Otherwise, they would get her married off and my mother had made the situation even more restrictive. We were put to test from either sides, but this phase had made us realize the intensity of the attachment that both of us had for each other.*

The channels of interaction were reduced to a minimum. There were no phone calls, no texts and complete detachment was forced on us even when I was home. During our rare visits, Neha stayed in complete isolation and I had to handle my heart on my own. No questions, no answers, no giggles; just blank faces, which were encountered accidentally. Mom started giving her her food in her room, rather than inviting her to eat with the family. She cooperated with Mom as she wanted the same. But breaking a budding relationship suddenly gives pain. I thought of calling her but dropped the idea, thinking about her enormous patience. The more I tried to ignore her, the more I was drawn to her. One day, this instability reached its peak.

I had come home for Diwali and we were busy preparing. Festivals are a medium to connect hearts and the same held true for us as well. She came out of her room and stood with us. I felt a change in Mom's behaviour that day. Maybe we had succeeded in gaining her confidence in the past few days. We stood on the rooftop and lit up earthen lamps. I was happy to see them talking to each other and laughing together after a long time. We tried to make eye contact, but couldn't succeed. In the past few days, I had realized her importance in my life. I had realized that she was my strength and her absence was screwing me over badly. I lost interest in my studies and my motivation was diminishing by the day. I decided to talk to her and take our relationship forward, as only that could rejuvenate my life.

'Hi Neha! Happy B'day!'

I texted her at midnight, sitting in my bedroom and expecting a reply from her. After few moments, I texted her again,

'Neha, it's already been 15 days, 22 hours since we talked last! Please say something, please! I am dying to talk to you, Neha.'

There was no reply and l felt the pain of losing her. The intensity of my love did not allow me to let her go. After about fifteen minutes, my phone vibrated. I immediately jumped to check it and the texting trail started.

Neha- Thanks Sunny. But how did you know?

Me- *How could I forget your birthday, Neha? That's ingrained in my heart.*

Neha- A small correction. It is 15 days, 21 hours since we talked last.

Me- Great! I thought you forget everything. I felt as if I am talking to a stranger.

Neha- I can't forget you Sunny... at least not in this life.

Me- I want to give a special gift to you.

Neha- Ohh really! What's that?

Me- Neha, I don't know where it goes and how it goes, but I can't stop the flutter in my heart anymore. I don't know whether it's right or wrong, but I can't resist this feeling anymore. I don't know whether we'll carry it forward or not, but now, I want to reveal what I am treasuring deep inside my heart. I love you Neha. I really do. And I mean it.

My heart was pounding hard to click the 'send' button. But finally, I gathered my wits and guts to press it. Time paused for a few moments and my heart skipped a few beats. I got scared. Maybe I shouldn't have done that, but there was no other way out. Was she angry? What happened to her? Why wasn't she replying?

Neha- Can you please come to my room Sunny… but… be very careful.

The ocean of anxiety burst inside me. I got frightened why she had called me to her room. Was she angry? I took a deep breath to calm down my heartbeats. I moved towards her room, being scared every minute. What I was doing? Was there anything wrong in going to a girl's room at midnight? Was I betraying my parents? But what was wrong in that? I would only be meeting her and I was not going to do anything else for sure. She is my friend and I can meet her. My feelings are pious. I entered her room. She stood there, looking directly into my eyes and walked to me. I did not know what was going to happen. She hugged me passionately and began crying. I hugged her and caressed her hair to calm her down.

"Sunny, I don't know what our future holds in store, but I feel like I can't live without you anymore. What should I do, Sunny? Tell me, what should I do?" she was weeping in a suppressed voice, wetting my T-shirt.

"Don't worry, Neha. Please don't cry. Today is your birthday. You should live this moment."

"Yes, Sunny. You have made my birthday so memorable by giving me the biggest gift of my life. Now, I can live with this feeling for the rest of my life, even if I have to survive without you. A man like you, loved me once. This feeling is enough for me to survive," she said with her moist eyes.

"Not just once. I love you Neha and I will love you forever. I assure you, we will unite someday, forever," I kissed her forehead. "Just have faith on Shiv ji. He'll manage everything." I winked to lighten her mood.

Industrial Visit

October 2011

"Your story is really very emotional bro, but I think you should rest now. We can finish it later. Have a good night's sleep." Ashu got off Sunny's bed to make him comfortable. He supported his back to lay him down, and placed a cushion beneath his head.

"Thanks bro," Sunny said in his emotionally overwhelmed voice.

Ashu smiled and said, "Anything for you bro. Now close your eyes and sleep."

Sunny thanked his stars for blessing him with such a great friend with whom he could share his emotional issues. Later that day, Ashu and Sunny got busy with their studies, as semester exams were around the corner. Sunny took two weeks to recover from the fracture and in the third week, his hand was plaster free. After a month, the college arranged an industrial visit for its students. In BHU, this visit was led by the seniors who pick up the most enthusiastic and smart juniors as assistants and showcase the talent of their college to industries to lure top-notch organizations for placements. This is done based on a rigorous selection process of presentations and interviews conducted by seniors and faculty members. Undoubtedly, Sunny and Ashu bagged this privileged opportunity.

Scene-1

Station

Finally the day arrived, after about twenty-five sleepless nights and restless days as part of the preparations. After all, it was directly affecting the reputation of the college. Everybody had to gather at the Varanasi station, to catch their respective trains. All of them took taxis to reach the station. It was a huge mob that accumulated on the roads of Banaras and it was more crowded than usual. Sunny asked the taxi driver why there was such a crowd, and he replied saying that it was because of the *pre-Shivratri* preparations that were going on around the city. Many times, the taxi driver kept saying while he was driving, "This year Shivratri is going to be very special babuji. It is falling on the same day as lunar eclipse." Since the day carried much religious significance, a huge assembly of people, families and ascetics from across the nation were expected to be visiting Banaras to witness the pomp and show of the celebrations. As the auto crawled on the roads, they noticed many hoardings put up that talked about the celebrations. Few temples were also renovated and the renovation process blocked many common roads of the city, leading to a pathetic traffic condition. All of this made it difficult to travel due to many dead ends and blockages on the road. Sunny and his friends were frightened that they might miss their train, but the prudence of the taxi driver saved them. He chose many shortest possible lanes and made them reach the station just fifteen minutes before the train departure. The Delhi gang was ready to catch the Shiv Ganga train. It was a group of around ten people including Ashu, Sunny and Ishita and a few other seniors. Everyone was busy gossiping about the trip. Suddenly, Sunny turned numb. He stopped reacting to the chatter going around, as he felt his nervous system getting disturbed. He had a fake smile on his face. His ears were not even listening to whatever his friends were saying, be it a matter of smile or shock. The reason that triggered this panic attack was the announcement of trains going to Bihar. He felt like he should run from there and board one of those trains. It was more than two years now that he had talked to her last. He did not know why, but he started looking around hastily, as if looking for someone.

"Hey Sunny, what happened? Looking for someone?" Ishita asked.

He did not say a word. It was as if he had not heard her, and suddenly, he ran away. He ran madly in the crowd, leaving all of them in a state of shock. Within a few minutes, he was out of their line of sight. It was like he had just seen her among the thousands of faces roaming around. He felt her presence there and he got a feeling that he had just seen those eyes. He was unsure what his eyes had just registered, but he did not want to lose that chance, even if the probability of she being there was least. As he entered the station, his mind was triggered to look for her. He visualized her stepping off one of the trains that came in from Bihar. This created such an impulsive response that he stepped into one of the trains going to Bihar just to confirm her presence. The time he took to confirm this took long enough and the train began moving. A sudden shock returned him to his senses and he jumped off the moving train, barely managing to save his legs. He checked his watch which showed two minutes remaining for his own train to leave for Delhi. He ran with double the speed and found Ashu midway, who was looking for him.

"You will be killed by me someday! Where had you gone?" Ashu yelled at him.

"Run bro, run!" Sunny yelled. They caught the train finally, boarding some random coach. Ashu's phone rang.

"Hello sir. Yes. We finally made it. Okay sir, Yeah... Yeah... no problem... Yes I am with him. Okay, bye," Ashu talked to Pawan on call.

"Bhai, you would have gotten both of us killed today. What is wrong with you, man? Your life is very important, bro! Do not put it at stake like that. Last time you had your arm broken. This time you would have broken your leg. Till when will it go on like this? And where did you run away at the eleventh hour?" Ashu said.

"I am sorry, bhai. I never want to put you in trouble, but it happens. I am very sorry this time. But, I think it will go like this until I find her," Sunny replied.

"Bhai, you are going to tell me the whole story today. Finally, we have enough time to chat and the journey is a long one. We will find a solution!" Ashu said.

"Sure bro. But let us move to our compartment first. Let's sit on our berths and after that I will proceed with the story-telling!" Sunny replied.

Scene-2

Love at Risk

We parted again after her birthday and Diwali. This time, it was different, as we exchanged our hearts to dive deep into the ocean of love. The emotion of love is above any other. Neither of us cared about the consequences, nor did we feel ashamed. We were flowing with emotions, treasured deep inside the caves of our hearts. This emotion is inexplicable; it is mesmerizing. It creates a situation, when even a ring tone can flutter your heart, and getting to hear her voice is the true pursuit of happiness. Our love life was going well. We called and texted, and deleted all the records too. The very next day, I had a message from Neha.

'Not any urgent issue, but certainly important. Give me a call at night!'

I called her that night.

"Hey Neha, are you okay? Why are you sounding so low?"

"Yes, honey, I am okay... but..." she said in a suppressed voice.

"But what, Neha? Tell me what happened? Did anyone say something or did I do anything wrong?"

"Nothing yaar, I am tensed about our future. Will my father allow us to be together? Will aunty accept me? Sometimes I feel that we should not have been in a relationship. I have lost aunty's affection, Sunny. I don't know why she thinks like I am enticing you unnecessarily! Everything seems to be so negative to me these days!"

"Calm down, Neha. What's wrong? What wrong did we do? We are just like very good friends and we want to spend our lives together. You don't worry about Mom. I'll take care of her and you'll see that she will love you even more."

I added, "Hmm... your dad is a big concern for me right now, I agree. But we'll handle that situation also together, when the right time comes. You do not have to worry, Neha, when I am with you. Let me know what problem you are facing in studies. If you think our relationship is disturbing it, then we can keep it on halt for some time."

"Halt?" she was astonished.

"We will minimize our communication, till we realize our dreams. Yaar, you'll never get such a compromising and flexible boyfriend, you see."

"That's true Sunny, but..." she said and I was fed up of her buts.

"No if, no but! Just do one thing," I commanded at her.

"Okay, as you say," she said and I heard a smile in her voice.

"Take a deep breath," I guided.

"Okay, taken," she said inhaling a big breath of fresh air inside.

"Blow out all the pressure on your phone now, by speaking out my name." I could hear the sharp blow of air on the other side of the phone in the next moment complemented with my name, spoken in the most sensuous way ever.

"How are you feeling now?"

"Hehe... I feel better now," she laughed. "Sunny. There is some sound in the porch. I think it is aunty. I will disconnect the call. Let us text now."

"Okay, no problem." She hung up. We shared a few texts that night and went to sleep.

Scene-3

Visit to Munger

"So tell me, where did you go on the day of our freshers' party?" Ashu asked. "Now, I have found an answer to your uninformed escape last time. You went to Bihar to meet bhabhi. Right?" he added. "And you still meet each other? Great!"

"Yes and no. Yes, for the first question and no for the second," Sunny said taking a deep breath. "I mean, I did go to Bihar in the hope of meeting your bhabhi, but I couldn't meet her," Sunny's voice turned heavy this time.

"So, you mean you are not in contact with her anymore?" His eyes popped out. Sunny smiled, masking the pain in his heart. "I thought that you went to meet her and she gave you this half pendant in return."

"No bro, the bitter fact is, even I don't know where she is!" Sunny said with pain reflecting in his eyes.

"Oh my god! Are you serious?" He was stupefied.

"Who did that to you? Your arm was fractured and you had many injuries! I thought her father or brother must have hit you, asking you to stay away from her."

"Bhai, that's another story in itself," Sunny replied.

"I want to know that story. Please, don't test my patience anymore," he uttered in frustration.

"We have not been in contact for the last two-and-a-half years. I'll tell you why later, but that day, I went to Bihar in search of her. I just had an idea that she resides in Munger, Bihar, with her family. I was not aware of the crime rate of that region before I visited the place. I reached Munger with a lot of hope to find my love. But that hope died because of a series of events that happened next. First I became the prey of pickpocketers that left me with no money in a new place. Somehow I managed to survive on an empty stomach and spent the day searching for her address. Moreover, who cares about hunger at such a time. I had just one goal, and the connection I was feeling with that place, the soil where my Neha had grown up, was infusing the fuel in me. Every portion of that land gave me a new hope of meeting her. Even a slick of thought that maybe I could see her charged me up. I didn't leave any person that came across without asking about her family's whereabouts. But the way people were staring at me made me uncomfortable and I turned apprehensive of another mishap. The day passed with diminishing hopes. Moneyless, the station seemed to be the best alternative to spend the night. The environment already grew intimidating and I was trying to cover that perilous journey to the station very cautiously. Midway I got surrounded by a bunch of robbers. They appeared to be teenagers but well equipped with some weapons like knives. I already told that I had nothing to give them, but it seemed they got really pissed off with their futile attempt. I didn't have energy go for a scuffle and hence cooperated with them and politely handed over my watch and blazer. But then they tried to snatch my life away from me." Sunny narrated while taking out the pendant from his t-shirt.

"Ohh! Now I got the reason behind your broken hand. You know, you are the first of your kind. You need to be revered by all the lovers. I have never met such a lover in my life. Where are your feet?" Ashu bowed down in reverence

"What are you doing, brother?" Sunny laughed and pulled his feet impulsively.

"Okay. Tell me what happened next. How did the love story go forward after that night's uninformed disconnection of your call?" Ashu quizzed curiously.

Acceptance or Refusal

Scene-1

Home Visit

About three days passed after that incident, and I did not get a call or text from Neha. I was worried about her as I did not know what had happened to her. Probably Mom must have eavesdropped that night and Neha must have landed in trouble by now. I kept sending her messages during those three days, but she did not reply to any. Many times, I got the feeling that she had fallen ill, but I was reluctant to call Mom and ask about her well-being. I spent that night tossing and turning in bed. Plenty of questions ate up my mind. What if Mom....? What would happen to her? The fear was so intense that I felt a lump in my throat and tears rolled down my cheeks. I could hear my heart throbbing, shattering the silence of my hostel room. What if I would be devoid of her love for my entire life? I struggled to survive on the deadly ticking of the clock, waiting for dawn to hit the windowpanes, that would bring a little hope. The fear was freaking me out from within and my hands were shaking even while sending simple texts to her. I typed 'Neha' on my phone. My mind faltered before pressing the send button. Finally, after deep thought, I pressed the button. My eyes were constantly fixed on my phone. 'Please god... one response... pleasssssseee!' I begged.

Suddenly, I got to see the innocent face of Abhi, conceiving a momentary feeling of shame somewhere inside me. What impression would I stamp on his mind, once he got to know about this episode, which was still beyond his knowledge? Will he ever respect me? Or will I be devoid of brotherly love as well? I caressed his hair whilst recalling the escapades and romps we had gone on together as children. Somewhere in my heart, I longed for all those moments. I cursed myself for destroying her life and her dreams. I found myself guilty for Mom's change in behaviour. I felt that it was because of me that Neha had to face the wrath of Mom. She may be devoid of the love of a family she was blessed with. May be the blessings from a family had turned into tantrums of hatred now.

'Oh god! Doesn't she deserve happiness in her life, being your true devotee? Forget about me, but at least think about that poor girl who has deep faith in you,' I mumbled.

Suddenly the phone vibrated. I was trembling in fear to know the truth.

Neha- Please don't text me, Sunny.

Me- What happened??

I texted her again with my trembling hands.

Neha- Our fear.... realized... please stop if you want to see me alive.

I turned numb. There was no movement in my body. How will we justify our act to our parents, and in what way will I justify my conduct? How could my eyes confront those fuming eyes of Mom, which were once filled with love and affection for me? I kept pondering upon the consequences. Why did I assume that everything would be fine? Why did I believe that things will run smooth? I am not doing anything wrong. But I was definitely spoiling the life of an innocent girl! I screamed suddenly, to stop my brain from exploding.

"What happened, Bhaiya? A nightmare?" Abhi asked in his half-sleepy state.

"No... nothing... Yeah must have been a nightmare," I stuttered in panic. The next morning, we were asked to start for home. It was supposed to be an urgent visit, but no reason was mentioned as the basis for this urgency.

"Bhaiyaa, mom is calling us. Yoohooo! It is time for good food, good study, sound sleep, and amazing badminton matches. Home is fun filled with peace and solace and life gets just so beautiful there," he said in excitement. I just nodded, as I didn't know how to react to Mom's urgently calling us to Dehradun.

"Are you not excited, Bhaiya?" he asked.

I nodded, stretching my lips as much as I could in an attempt to contrive a fake smile.

"Okay! Great! We should pack our bags then," he said and moved into the room.

'Should I tell him the truth?' I wondered. But, his excitement made me reluctant. I knew he would be disappointed if he knew the truth. We packed our bags and took a taxi to the bus stand. After a lot of struggle, we managed to catch a bus headed for Dehradun. Thank god that Abhi was sleeping for the entire journey with his ear-phones plugged in. Thoughts kept crawling in my mind as the wheels of bus kept turning, and they did not even let me take a nap. After a round of rigorous brainstorming, finally, I made up my mind to face the situation with the truth.

I decided that I wouldn't dress up the situation, nor lie. But I would face it as it was, in the way it came to me. I thought of expressing my honest feelings that my heart was pining for Neha. Maybe that would make my life easier. After around two hours on the bus, and ten minutes in the taxi, we landed up at the entrance of our colony with our backpacks.

The board said 'Shakti Vihar Colony' and a huge black gate welcomed us. We entered inside with totally opposite feelings – one was so light that he was flying in ecstasy and the other was immobile with the burden of guilt and gloom. As the way to our home grew shorter, the pressure inside grew. It was killing me. I couldn't figure out how Abhi would feel when he got to know the truth. This was something I had been hiding from him for a significant amount of time. He, being a close friend of mine, would be upset at my not telling him this in the first place. Secondly, he would be upset for having chosen our friend's sister, for that matter. Things were getting worse for me with every passing second and fate was giving me another reason to feel guilty and sad about.

"Bhaiya! Neha will also be excited by our surprise visit! Only if..." he paused and then continued, "...I hope you haven't leaked the news to her. Have you?"

I just shook my head with a restrained smile. "Mom!" Abhi yelled, unlocking the gate. We heard her approaching steps and the sound of the inner door being opened.

"Hello, my sons!" Mom hugged us tight and we bowed down to touch her feet. Her expressions did not reflect anything abnormal. Maybe she wanted to deal with it prudently. While walking through the alley, my steps involuntarily slowed down beside Neha's room. It was closed, and no ray of light was seen. Only a small line between the curtains of the long window were

seen. I prayed to god to flutter the curtains slightly, to let me look at her at least once, but no luck. We moved inside and greeted dad. He was working at his desk. He turned around and threw a glance at both us.

"Hello boys! How was your journey?" he asked.

"It was okay Papa. A little tiring!" Abhi said.

"So what's up? Anything exciting?" he asked, looking at me with an inquisitive smile.

"Yes Papa! Our Head of Electronics Department, Vipul sir, is impressed with my semiconductors project," Abhi said.

"Oh, great. Sunny, how are your preparations going?" Papa asked.

"It is go... ing... fine," I replied.

"You sure?" his eyes widened and eyebrows jumped slightly as if expecting a different answer. I just nodded. I could clearly sense that the reason for our urgent visit was something that had to do with me.

Scene-2

Discussion

Every second passed by like months for me, as I was going through the dreaded waiting period for the trial. I sat in my room, swinging like a pendulum between the two extremities of the consequences. My mind was crushed with the thoughts of our departure, that escalated more with her absence. Four hours had passed since we had reached home and I could not even see her. This was not normal. Earlier, she used to come running with Mom, with her cheerful smile and glittering eyes. I could imagine her the same way, but with tears flowing down her cheeks this time. I rehearsed the situation in my mind, wondering what I was about to face, speculating the questions that could be fired at me and conjecturing possible euphemistic answers. This was not a normal interview for me as I could not afford to lose. The only possibility was to crack the interview as I had to win my love. I had to put my strongest efforts to crack it, because it was not meant only for me, but also for her. I felt guilty for causing my mother so much pain. I did not want to trouble my mom, but I placated my heart by saying that 'I was giving her the best daughter-in-law in the world, the one who would take care of her, forever.' Finally, the long awaited moment arrived at 5:00 p.m. when Abhi went out for badminton practice. Papa came to my room and asked me to come to the living room.

"Yes Papa, coming," I replied. My heart was pounding so fast, I stood up impulsively, dropping my food.

"What happened?" Papa asked, turning around.

"Nothing Papa, it's just this plate," I stooped down on my knees to pick the plate up, and the food I had dropped.

"Beta, your mom gave you lunch three hours ago, and you have not eaten a morsel yet!" Papa was shocked to see me like that.

"It's okay, Papa. I am fine!" I kept brushing the floor to collect every particle in the plate. I did not look at him, as I wanted to hide my tears.

"Beta, I don't think so. Come, let's have a talk. I think it is necessary now," he said and moved away swiftly. After I finished cleaning, I moved to the living room. My steps had turned into baby steps and I was reluctant to enter the room. But as I reached, I clenched my fist, and gave a thrust to my legs. Mom and Dad were muttering between themselves, while sitting on the sofa. They were sipping their evening tea, and stopped talking as soon as I entered.

"Come, Sunny!" Mom said. Her voice sounded a little authoritative this time and marked her demeanour. My legs had lost all strength. I entered the living room silently with sealed lips. I sat on the chair right in front of their sofa. I kept my head down, waiting for them to trigger the conversation.

"Sunny, I hope you already know why we are here," she said with a tinge of sharpness in her voice. This was Mom's characteristic; she would come straight to the point, without beating around the bush. I nodded and tried making eye contact with her, but I could not. "I warned you earlier, Sunny. I did not expect this from you. How could you do this? You did not think about us even once? We are sheltering someone's dignity and pride and we are supposed to protect that. You have broken our trust, Sunny. You pricked that faith – the faith of friendship that you shared with Rohan, the faith that's the heart of every relationship; a son, a brother, a friend. It's a shame for all of us!" Her pitch rose and her face turned red.

Papa placed his hand on her shoulder and caressed her to calm her down, as he could notice her rising blood pressure.

"Yes Mom! I broke your trust and I definitely played with your faith. If giving support to someone is against someone's faith, then I have broken it definitely. If giving love to someone who is devoid of it is against someone's faith, then I have lost that faith, Mom! If wiping someone else's tears is against someone's faith, then I have definitely committed a crime. Yes, I have broken your trust Mom no doubt about that," I said with a trembling voice.

"I am not demeaning these 'acts' but the 'intentions' behind them, Sunny. You can do all this as a 'brother' as well," she said, making a gesture using her fingers just to emphasize her words.

"Brother? Oh god! Tell me one thing, Mom. Do you think that relationships and feelings can be infused in your blood forcefully? Or they can be scaled within the parameters of brother or father or lover or well-wisher or whatever else? You think you can modulate your feelings just the way you play with your furniture in the drawing room? Place the sofa here today, change the position of the table, replace it, put it somewhere else, remove it? Do you really think it happens, Mom? I don't think so. Feelings are guided by the heart, Mom, and not by words. All I know is, when she cries, I cry. When she feels pain, it stings me, and when she smiles, I smile. I just want the same feelings for her, forever," I said, looking into her eyes. Everything came straight from my heart and I did not mince words even a bit.

"Beta, I understand your feelings. But you cannot expect anything to exist for a lifetime. We are a part of society and we need to follow certain norms. Your decisions are influenced by the rules of society you live in. There is a right time for everything, Sunny. It always turns out to be reason to repent later, to tie your feet now with the shackles of lifetime commitments, when you haven't even secured your future. There can be a lot of better opportunities waiting to unravel themselves. You cannot make a decision, being drowned in emotions now. Mark my words Sunny, everything has its right time!" Papa said, sounding convincing rather than authoritative.

"I am sorry, Papa. I can't believe you are saying this. A person who moved out of his village breaching all orthodox notions and leaving all sorts of stereotypes behind is talking like this? I cannot believe it. I agree with your view, Papa, that there is a right time for everything and I will certainly wait for that moment. I know my responsibilities, Papa, and I'll definitely

stand by them. After all, I am your son. But, you only told me once that one should follow his heart before it's too late. I am just following my heart Papa! I... I.... really love her... but that doesn't mean that I am escaping from my responsibilities... or that I am running away from my dreams, career or anything of that sort. I'll fulfill my responsibilities towards you and then think about settling down with her. I am not like those cowards who snatch their love away from the world, leaving their loved ones to cry and crush their expectations, hopes and dreams. I don't want to snatch away my love, Papa, but I want to earn it. I will fulfill my duties first, and then would think of settling down with her."

"A very good speech, Sunny, I must say. I cannot allow you to love her. Not now, and not even in the future! Never! Do you understand that?" Mom said.

"Please talk softly, Mom, or she will hear you!" I stood up to close the door tightly.

"I don't care about that. I can speak the same way even in front of her. How could she even think of becoming your bride? I did so much for her and she is playing with my emotions and stabbing me behind my back."

"Mom! Please talk softly," I almost went down on my knees to plead with her.

"Yeah....Very good.... I cannot even speak what she did and she can do all that... make castles in air about her future... enticing my son... and doing everything that I don't like," Mom's anger was turning into tantrums of hatred now.

"Okay Mom! For god's sake, leave it, please!"

"Okay Sunny! For my sake, leave her, please!" Mom rhymed her words to mine. She played the trick as she knew that she could easily blackmail me in the name of my emotions for.

"Okay. But only on one condition, that you will not say a single bitter word in front of her. It's not about her Mom, it is about me. She has been drowned into this painful lane by me. I'll not forgive myself if she gets hurt. But tell me, what made your lovely heart hate her so badly? You touched her heart with your tender love, but what made you change completely now? I want an answer, Mom. Give me the answer!" I bent my head on her knees and started crying.

After a pause, I felt her fingers running in my hair, caressing my head softly. She was polite. Maybe a mother's heart had taken over, which could not stand to see her son crying before her. She took a deep breath and tried to regain her composure.

"Beta, I don't want to hurt your feelings, but you have to understand that I am doing all this only for you. Perhaps you'll understand later. I am trying to provide her the best in this house. But I definitely cannot see her as my daughter-in law," Mom cupped my face and it seemed she had hypnotized me with her teary eyes. I could see her lips quivering in pain, and she was just about to cry. I surrendered myself looking at Mom's state.

"Okay, Mom. If it makes you happy, I will follow what you say. Please don't say anything to her. Let her study for her exams," I requested half-heartedly.

"I promise, beta. I'll give her even more love than before," she said. I made my sacrifice without thinking of the aftermath. Those were my vulnerable moments. On the one hand, it was Mom; on the other, it was Neha. I had to choose one and by no means could I afford to lose Mom. Even Neha would have hated me had I done that.

Scene-3

The Ephemeral Acceptance

The pain of sacrifice reduces when you realize it is for someone you love.

I sacrificed my tears for Mom's mental peace, and for Neha's dream, equally. We were completely insulated from each other, irrespective of my location, be it Haridwar or Dehradun. It was even more painful to stay under one roof and stay insulated while dying within for accidental glances, yearning for some mode of opportune communication. I did not know what was told to her and how she was managing her pain. But she was managing better than me. For me, it was getting intolerable by the day. I thought initially that I would manage without talking to her. But I was wrong to have believed that. One day, Mom went to her room, just to have a small chat with her.

"Neha, how are you beta?" Mom asked in a cheerful tone, taking a glass of water and a pack of tablets with her. She was happy to take care of her, as long as I was away.

"I am fine, Aunty!" she said, reciprocating with a smile, while lying on her bed. She was studying, and had her book on her face.

"So, studying? Hmm...." Mom caressed her hair. The promise I gave to Mom had appeased her soul. Her behaviour towards Neha had changed back to normal.

"Yes Aunty!" Neha nodded and asked about my well-being. We had promised Mom that only she would play the role of a communication channel between us. We could just ask about each other's well-being, at least for a month or so, which was supposed to be a period of recovery, according to Mom.

"He is okay. Don't worry. I am taking good care of him," she replied.

"If he asks about me, Aunty, please don't tell him I am ill. He is very sensitive. Please take care of him. Ah... sorry Aunty, who am I to tell you this? You are his mom. You are more concerned about him," she tried to express her concern for me.

Mom's expressions changed immediately. She was astonished to see such care for me in her eyes. Lying unwell in bed herself, she was more worried about me and my pain. How could someone care about somebody else to such an extent! The warmth of her words touched Mom's heart, but was not enough to change her mind. There was a strong reason in her heart which was not letting her accept Neha.

"Okay, beta! I will not tell him. But take your medicines on time. Last night, I was really scared to see your high temperature!" Mom said politely.

"Okay. Thanks for your concern, Aunty."

"Beta, I am not your enemy. I really care for both of you. But just a few things are beyond my control. I hope you understand. If not now, maybe later. Once you become a mother, you will recall my words," Mom replied, gazing into her eyes with affection.

"I understand Aunty..." She coughed.

"Beta, you just rest. Do let me know if you need anything." Mom tapped her back gently. Later in the afternoon, the same day, I called Mom.

"Hello Mom."

"Yes beta!" Mom greeted me cheerfully.

"Mom!" I coughed.

"Hey! What happened?" she asked.

"Nothing Mom, just cold and fever," I replied in a low tone.

"Mom! He had extremely high temperature last night and I took him to the University dispensary. Now he seems to be okay, Ma!" Abhi yelled, snatching the phone from me.

"Ohh beta! Why didn't you tell me till now? Come here. I'll take care of you. You will be perfectly alright, my son!" she responded in concern. I grabbed the phone back from Abhi and moved away.

"No Mom, I am okay! If I come, maybe she would come to know about my health and get disturbed. I don't want that to happen at all. Please Mom, she should not know about it. You know she is sensitive. The worst part is, she won't even be allowed to see me."

"Okay, beta! I'll..." her voice turned heavy, as if she was unable to find words.

"Mom! May I ask you how she is? Please take care of her, Mom. That's a request and a part of our deal as well."

"Don't worry about that, Sunny. You take care of yourself. That's it. Do not hesitate to come here if needed. This is my request and part of our deal too. Hand over the phone to Abhi. I think I have to straighten him out now, to take due care of you," she spoke strictly. After a few days, I visited Dehradun. One day, when I was studying on the terrace, I suddenly sensed a shadow lurking behind me. I wiped away my tears as I saw Mom approaching me.

"Beta," she rested her palm on my head.

"Yes Mom? The weather is so good here. The warm sun during winter, such a soothing combination. Right Mom?" I tried to escape her glare.

"Hmm... I can see that. But I don't think it is sunny enough to dry your tears away," she said.

"Please let me study, Mom! Sine theta and cos..." I tried to free myself from the conversation. She pulled up a chair and sat beside me.

"Beta, I thought you could handle it. You were and you are a strong boy... but..." she said, gazing into my eyes.

"It's okay, Mom. Sometimes... It happens... Don't worry! I will handle it," I replied.

"Beta, I have waited for a month, keeping an eye on the both of you. I was wrong. Both of you just keep asking about each other, sacrificing your own happiness only for me. I can't handle it anymore, beta. I am also a human, and I have a heart too. Beta, I cannot put you both in pain anymore. I just want the both of you to be happy!" she added.

"Mom! What are you saying? What does that mean?" I turned to face her, just to hear what my mind had already made out.

"It's true beta. Please promise me first, though, that you will not let this impact your career. That's the only concern which eats me nowadays. I was scared, beta, as I have seen my own brother spoiling his career," she said with her voice trembling.

"Yes, Mom! I promise! I'll definitely fulfill your dreams. Thank you so much, Mom. I love you. I really love you. Thank you so much for understanding our love, Mom. You'll see how I make you proud now. I owe my life to you, my lovely Mom!" I hugged her tightly, like I used to in my childhood.

"Okay, my son! Concentrate on your studies now," she said with a smile. "And yes beta! You were right. The weather is very pleasant today. Sunny enough to dispel the dust of ego out of my mind," she added.

"... And sunny enough to wipe away my tears, Mom!" I replied and we smiled.

Scene-4

The First Kiss

It was like a dream come true, that too in the twinkling of an eye. My senses were going out of control, after realizing the thin line between dream and reality. I was jumping. I was excited about sharing this moment of ecstasy with my love after a prolonged phase of despair and separation. I ran towards her room jumping off the staircase, skipping three to four of steps in a go.

"Beta, be careful!" Mom yelled as she heard a loud thudding sound.

"Yes, Mom! I am fine," I responded. I stopped when I was about to reach her room. My heartbeat was too fast and I gasped to calm my breath down. It's a beautiful and an ironic creation of nature that the symptoms – increased heartbeats, wet eyes, which happen in both the extremities of emotions, happiness and sorrow – raise exactly the opposite feelings in us. I knocked at her door. I thought of taking her in the air and dancing as soon as I saw her. The door opened and it was after a painful gap of ten days that I was seeing her.

"Oh, Sunny!" A momentary smile appeared on her lips which immediately vanished with an extreme fear.

"Please go away. Where is Aunty? Please go. I promised her, please for god's sake Sunny... Go!" she said changing her expressions within seconds.

I moved inside without saying a word and kept moving towards her. She walked backwards, scared. I gazed into her eyes with a smile and moved forward as if I was feeling happy about teasing her.

"Please Sunny! Go away from here. What are you doing? Don't spoil my life, please, Sunny. I can't handle it anymore,"

she cried, moving backwards. She kept speaking continuously, without even listening to me.

"Mom has accepted our love," I broke the news and thus, my silence too.

She kept speaking continuously, without even paying heed to my words, "Please Sunny, let me study now. I made a mistake... that..." suddenly she stopped. "What? What did you just say?" she asked me.

"Yes, Mom has accepted our love and I am here only on her discretion," I said, smiling.

"No! You are a liar. I don't believe you. Please do not play with my emotions. I can't bear it anymore. You are a liar, Sunny, you are a liar! You are a liar! L...iaarrrrr!" she began punching my chest hard.

"It is true," I held her hand and looked straight into her eyes. She reciprocated the same meditative gaze at me. Her eyes were innocent, filled with tears, but with the tears of hope this time.

"Really?" her voice softened. Her expressions changed to those of happiness, and we remained connected through our eyes. It was indeed a meditative connection. I moved my face towards hers. It was an automated movement in the flow of extreme emotions. I did not do it deliberately. As my lips came closer to hers, she just closed her eyes as if she had surrendered herself to me. My lips touched hers, gracefully, taking hers into mine, with an extreme flush of emotions and arousal. I felt like I was kissing the soft petals of a moistened rose. I noticed her lip movements after a little phase of reluctance, as if she had also gotten drowned in the same emotion. We experienced the meditative state of love, and the bliss. I felt the pious emotional connection that a kiss plays between two souls, for the very first time. The sudden movement of steps shook us out of the stupor. We straightened ourselves. Her face was blushing with shyness

and she was not letting her eyes meet mine. I found her a little coy. Suddenly, that kiss had made her feel like a woman.

"Abhemmm... May I come in?" Mom asked knocking at the door.

"Obviously, Mom. Please don't embarrass us," I replied turning towards her. Neha immediately grabbed her place on the bed.

"Yes, Aunty!"

"Neha, so Sunny has told you?" Mom asked. She just smiled a shy smile in response. "Look at her Sunny, she is blushing."

"Yes Mom! She's been like that since I told her."

"Are you happy now, beta? I pondered a lot, spending many sleepless nights, thinking about the both of you. The care and love you have for each other has moulded me to take this decision. What future am I securing for my son, if I am killing his present?" Mom said, caressing Neha's hair.

"Thank you Aunty. Thanks a lot. I love you. I promise you, Aunty, that I'll be a good daughter-in-law!" she said, hugging her tightly.

"And the best wife as well!" I said, cuddling the both of them. I went back to Haridwar after that day to resume my studies and we continued our telephonic conversations, as before. Our love story was at its peak after Mom's approval. We swayed in air like free love birds, weaving dreams for our wedding and life after it. Neha would sometimes tell me how grand she wanted the wedding to be and how she wanted to buy gold jewellery for herself as she had never bought any in her life. Every day, she would share a new wish about our wedding and our life together. Every day, she would make me fall in love with her even more, because of her longing and excitement to be married to me. She was excited about her wedding lehenga, her sarees,

all the customs and traditions of our family, when she would be coming to our house as the eldest bride of our family. She said she wanted to garland me, standing on the rotating stage that was now a trending fashion. She had been excited about getting married right from her childhood days, because she knew that was the only time a girl is allowed to spend lavishly on herself. She was fond of make-up and she knew that her wedding day was the only time when she could look her best. She wanted to book a luxurious Lakme bridal make-up for her D-day. For me, other than getting to listen to her voice, it was exciting to call her every day and know what new wish she had woven. I was living my dreams in her wishes and my excitement in her cheerfulness. She made me mad about her, talking about the kind of feelings she would have, when I would tie the mangalsutra around her neck and apply sindoor in her hair parting.

A woman gets more excited about everything that completes her as a woman! When she was busy making plans for our wedding, I was pondering about our honeymoon and golden night. We were both weaving dreams but the state of mind was different. She thought about the dresses and jewellery, while I was thinking of innovative ways to undo them. She was concerned about the kind of flowers to be used for garlands, while I was worried about the kind of flowers to be used on our bed on our golden night. That is the difference between male and female psychology.

Scene-5

The Game of Expectations

We began treating ourselves as husband and wife and behaving in the same way. All her morning calls were complemented with good mornings, spoken like a spouse would. Our conversations became more meaningful, and concentrated on our future. We talked about which city we wanted to settle in, when to buy our first car and where to send our kids for school. We noticed the changes in our behaviour, but it was Neha who was more affected by this change. The way she greeted me and acknowledged my opinions were all changing. I realized how a girl's perspective changes once her heart acknowledges someone as her husband. It was strange to notice, but she was like that. Maybe it is because of the environment she was brought up in that made her act coy. On one end, our love life was blossoming in full-swing, but on the other hand, the dragon of expectations was waiting to swallow our love life. One day, when Mom was sharing tea with her best friend from the locality Mrs Shukla, they landed up talking about something strange.

"Ohh Mrs Sharma, you are so funny sometimes!" their giggles and chortles were echoing in the house.

"I have learnt this from you only, Mrs Shukla!" Mom added. Neha walked past their room and thought of greeting Mrs Shukla as she had come home after a long time.

"Hello Aunty! How are you? And how is Uncle?"

"Everything is fine Neha. So, how are your studies going?"

"Good, Aunty."

"That is good Neha, when is your CAT exam?" aunty asked Neha.

"After two months, Aunty!" Neha said.

"Good! So beta, what are your future plans? MBA then marriage... hmm?"

"Hmm... I think so, Aunty."

"Beta MBA and all is fine... But home management is something one needs to learn. How good are you in that, cooking and all that stuff?"

"Hehe... cooking? I know how to cook egg-bhurji, Aunty!" Neha laughed.

"Yuck! Ram Ram! You know, you are a paying guest at a Brahmin household. You are not even allowed to utter such words."

"I am sorry, Aunty. But you know the biscuit you are eating also has egg as an ingredient. Not just this, but most of our daily routine usage edibles contain animal extracts."

Mrs Shukla spat out the chewed morsel immediately. "Is it true, Mrs Sharma?"

"I don't know. It's your favourite one," Mom replied, looking at Mrs Shukla, confused.

"Okay, Aunty! I have to go to study now." Mrs Shukla smiled an embarrassing smile at Neha. Neha went back to her room to resume her studies after her witty retorts.

"You really have a magnanimous heart, Mrs Sharma, I must say. You have sheltered a girl like her in your home. You know they are 'Kayastha', who eat a lot of non-vegetarian food. Has she ever lent you a hand in cooking?"

"No!" Mom replied hesitantly.

"Don't let her do that. She'll herself never lend it to you anyway, she doesn't even know how to cook! Even if you allow her to do it, you do not know what she will cook for pious people like you and your husband. She will spoil your religious practices, trust me. Allowing her to stay at your place for her studies is still acceptable, Mrs Sharma, but letting her cook will force me to believe that you are not wise," she said and Mom nodded with an uncomfortable smile.

"I feel sympathetic about the unfortunate family she'll get married into, Mrs Sharma. She doesn't even know the 'A' of home management. No cooking, no dressing sense at all. She

does not know how to carry herself and be presentable. She is so feeble and frail, that I have seen her legs shivering sometimes when she stands. I can bet that she must have some hormonal problems too. What happened that day when you took her to doctor?"

Mrs Shukla executed a fantastic plot with her awesome communication skills to convince Mom that she had committed the biggest mistake of her life.

"Hmm... That doctor doesn't seem to be good to me," Mom replied, leaning back in the sofa.

"Good? He is the best doctor in the city. I know what she would have said! She told me as well, once," Shukla Aunty threw another trap at Mom.

"Has she told you?" Mom's eyes popped out.

"I mean, I know, I am also half a doctor myself. Neha can never get pregnant. She cannot conceive. The doctor must have told you the same thing, right?" Shukla Aunty did not spare a second thought before speaking those words.

"Ahhmm... yaa she told me the same...." Mom said, bending her head down.

"Mrs Sharma! You are innocent like a cow. Does anyone, who is having eligible bachelors in the family, shelter such a so-called well-behaved girl at home? You have taken an extremely dangerous and risky decision, I must say. But thank god, I know your sons are far smarter than what you are. They will not be affected or cajoled by any girl, especially Sunny. He is too mature and I know his choice. He likes my Tanu, I know it very well." She smiled.

"Hmm... Ahhh! Okay!" Mom said gesturing a fake smile, totally ignorant about the trap Shukla Aunty had thrown at her to fall into.

"Both of them talk a lot on the phone and you know the young generation today!" She laughed again.

"Okay. I should leave now, Mrs Sharma." Shukla Aunty felt that her purpose was accomplished. She stood up, arranging her saree; she moved towards the kitchen to place the cups back. Mom escorted her, taking along the tray of biscuits and used plates.

Mrs Shukla saw something in the kitchen and asked, "See... this plate is her's right? I am shocked. What kind of family does she belong to? Nobody taught her any etiquette. She could have washed it after eating."

"What to say, Mrs Shukla! Youngsters are like that these days. They have to study and they are so busy that they cannot make time for such menial tasks. It is okay, I will wash them!" Mom tried to cover up Neha's ignorance.

"No, Mrs Sharma. I'll not tolerate if my Tanu does anything of that sort. At least at somebody else's place. This is not a part of my upbringing. I have educated my Tanu to behave well with her other family." Shukla Aunty left no stone unturned to demean Neha in Mom's mindset.

Suddenly, Neha entered the kitchen, with her used plate and started washing it in the sink.

"Aunty, sorry! I forgot to tell you. Tanu had come in the afternoon to meet me, and she was hungry, so I gave her some rice and dal. May I wash her used plates a bit later? I am little busy with my preparations for exams now." Neha truly lived the proverb of striking the iron when it is hot.

She was like that – bold, frank and upfront, except before my family members.

"No beta. It's okay! I'll do it," Mom said to her.

"Thanks Aunty!" she said and moved to her room. "Excuse me Aunty!" she carved her way between Mom and Mrs Shukla. Mrs Shukla turned around, speechless.

Neha walked ahead and then turned around. "Aunty! Don't worry! I think Tanu must have been in a hurry. I know you have inculcated these etiquettes in her; you are a great mom and you have raised your children so well, we all know that." She smiled and went back to her room. Mrs Shukla left hastily, realizing that she had been insulted.

Scene-6

Disappointment

Everything went fine for the next couple of days, but suddenly something happened which shook our rosy world.

"What happened, Neha? You sound so low again," I asked, after listening to her answer the phone.

"I don't know, Sunny, I am feeling very lonely here... I feel suffocated... I want to go back home."

"Go home? Why are you saying that? Please tell me, Neha. What happened?"

"Sunny! I feel that Aunty doesn't like me at all. She keeps crying every time, repeating the same words over and over again that she has destroyed her son's life by keeping a girl at her home. Am I that bad, Sunny?" Neha asked me.

"No, Neha! I know she worries about my career often, and feels that I am diverting my attention towards you instead of concentrating on my studies and my career. That's probably why she says so. It doesn't matter whether it is you or someone else. There is no other reason for her to be worried about, but my career. Don't feel bad, Neha!" I tried to placate her.

"Sunny, for the past few days, the situation has worsened. I don't know what Mrs Shukla says to aunty, and what your relatives do. All I know is that she is going into depression all

because of me. Sometimes, I feel that she cries more whenever I am around. Maybe she wants me to refuse to marry you myself, watching her bad condition and her tantrums. I also come from a good family Sunny, and..." Neha stopped in between and it seemed she had started sobbing.

"I know that, Neha. In fact, we all know that. But how are these things getting into our conversation, just out of the blue?" I spoke worriedly.

"No, Sunny. It was tolerable for as long as it was restricted to me, but now, I can't tolerate a word against my family," Neha confessed and it shook me from within. I could not believe that Mom had started talking ill about her family also.

"Who says what about your family, Neha? Tell me," I asked half-heartedly.

"It may not be done directly, Sunny, but I am no fool to miss the subtle hints. Mrs Shukla and Mummy indirectly talk about... my fami...." she burst into tears.

"Don't bother about Mrs Shukla, Neha! She is a fool. She is the culprit behind all this. Please stop crying, please!" I tried making all efforts to appease her, but I could not succeed. For the first time, I realized how tough it would be for people in long-distance relationships to survive, and keep their relationships intact.

"I am not bothered about her, but she has completely brainwashed your Mom! That's why she behaves like... I can't say it! Enough, Sunny! I can't stay in this house anymore. Aunty thinks bad about me and my family, she has started expecting so much from me! Our life will be hell Sunny!" She started crying loudly.

I cut her short and said, "Please don't feel this way, Neha. It is natural. She has accepted you as my bride, so it is obvious that expectations will grow by the day. Don't worry, it's just a matter of a few days and then you are going back to your hometown. We have to live a long phase of separation to fulfill our dreams, and then to win our love back! We must be patient, Neha. If you lose hope like this, how will we fight the battle to be together forever? Ignore all this. Mom will be fine with time!" I made the best possible answer to assuage her.

"Okay, Sunny. I don't know how I will survive without you," she said.

"Don't worry Tuntun.... Our love will infuse strength inside us."

"Tuntun?" she spoke in surprise and added. "You give me a new name almost every other day."

"It is because you are just like a baby. Now, will you please open the petals of your gorgeous rose-like lips, and give me my share of sweetness?"

"Hmm. Sometimes I feel that you are very proficient in dealing with girls. How many girls have you enticed with your hypnotic, honey-coated words so far?"

"Uh... 1... 2... 3... 4.... ahh...4th one was no... no... she was... ahh... 3 and a half!" I replied, faking some calculations.

"Three-and-a-half? What's that?" she asked, laughing.

"Actually the fourth one was sharing two boyfriends, including me... so evaluating that... I got half as a share!"

"Oh my god! So, I am the fifth! My friend was right. She had asked me never to believe Dehraduni boys. How could I!" she said, giggling.

"I was just joking!" I replied.

"Seriously?" she asked.

"I was lying... you are actually the 6th," I teased her again. She started crying like a child.

Scene-7

Fear

After that day, the complaints began about Mom's mood fluctuations. Neha was confused about her attitude and was unsure if she was happy with her or was disappointed. Sometimes, she felt affection and she would tell me about the care that Mom had bestowed on her. But some other times, it would be a complete contrast. One day, she informed me that Mom had brought her warm woollen innerwear, because she was shivering at night and the other day she commented on her being less immune to winter. It was a phase of bewilderment and I was caught between the two women. I consoled both of them and made fake stories to sow the seeds of love between both of them, as both of them were important to me. One evening, I stood on the terrace of my hostel to chat with Neha.

"I can understand, Neha. But please don't cry. At least be grateful to destiny that we are together. Just imagine what would have happened if Mom hadn't accepted it. Also, big thanks to technology, that we are connected somehow," I said.

"So, you will not come to Dehradun the day I'll be going, right?" she asked me.

"What should I say, Neha? You know that Mom has agreed on these terms only," I replied.

"What terms, Sunny? I am sorry, but I think your Mom is making fools out of us. What is this? Is there any logic to the fact that she has agreed to our wedding and that we can't see each other till then? Are you fine with this? Can you let me go without meeting me? I can't go like this Sunny. Until I wet your shoulders with my tears." She was furious.

"Okay, baba. I'll try!" I said, wondering how I'd execute it.

"Try?" She got even more furious this time.

"I mean I'll come..."

"You... betterrrr..."

Suddenly Mom snatched her phone away from her.

"Sunny, this is enough! I have been observing both of you talking for the last two hours. Is this the way you are going to keep my promise? Remember, I agreed upon some conditions. Make yourself eligible for this first, by settling down with a good career. Only after that will I allow you to proceed to the next step. Are you going to do it this way? Talking for hours and crying on the phone? What will you do when she'll be gone? I was scared of this. You'll spoil your life, Sunny. And I'll keep repenting my whole life for letting a girl stay in my home."

I could hear Neha crying in the background. "Mom... Please! What has happened to you? She is crying and you are speaking like that in front of her. This is not good, Mom. Please understand our situation," I pleaded.

"Okay, beta! You can't see her crying, but your Mom can cry before you. Is that it?" Mom was equally furious, as was Neha.

"I did not mean that, Mom. Please don't make a scene there. You should understand a girl's heart as well, Ma. She is going back after a week and has to take her exams. Why don't you understand that? What's the problem if I meet her once, before she leaves?"

"You are right, beta. I am the culprit here. I don't understand anything. I am a fool who just keeps caring about everyone. This girl has done something to our family. There was so much of love between us earlier, and now everybody takes her side. This girl has made everyone do her will with her black magic."

"Please Mom. Everybody cares for you. Please for god's sake. I'll go mad, Mom... stop saying that," I said and then I

disconnected the call. I got scared with what was happening. Suddenly, I realized that whatever Neha said to me was more horrific than what I had assumed. Mom seemed to have gone into a phase of depression and the reason was my career. But, really? Was that the only reason? Or was there something else aggravating her fear? I pondered over it a lot, that she would have behaved in the same way had there been some other girl instead of Neha. Maybe she was scared of the wrath of society, on moral and ethical grounds. Or scared that it would bring her dignity down, which she had earned after a life-long struggle, or maybe she thought I was wasting my life in this affair. Later that day, Abhi came to know about all this because of Mom's ill health and he gave me an uncanny reaction. He didn't say a word to me except, "You have broken the trust of every relation... a friend, a son and a brother. I am ashamed of you."

After that, he stopped talking to me. That was another intolerable setback for me. The bond of every relation was fading away, leaving a dreaded feeling of loneliness inside. There was no one who could understand my pain. Have I done anything wrong by loving that girl? I do not know, but it snatched everything away from me. Just a few months ago, my life was full of happiness, excitement and hope. And just one decision ruined our lives. The situation worsened drastically by the hour, as if somebody had cursed my fate.

I was getting ready for college in the morning one day. Suddenly my phone rang. "Hello!"

"Beta! How are you? Please come here, beta. I want to see you," Mom said to me in a broken voice.

"Yeah, Mom. I am coming. Don't worry. But, tell me, what has happened?" I asked, curious about her sudden change of mind.

"Nothing. Just feeling lonely. Want to see you, my son!" She was sounding really low and that scared the hell out of me.

"Why Mom? Is everything alright?" I kept probing her even more.

"Hmm. I am sorry, beta. I behaved very badly that day. Please pardon me and come here..."

"Nothing to be sorry about, Mom. It happens. That's not a problem. You just take care of yourself," I said, feeling sorry for her.

"Beta! I feel like I am troubling you a lot these days. I feel that I give you a lot of pain. Do whatever you wish, beta, I just want to see you happy. Come beta! Please come and see your Mom."

"Please Mom! Do not blame yourself for anything. I love you the most. If you seriously want me to come, I'll come, but don't call me just for the sake of my happiness," I requested her again.

"No, beta! I am calling you for my happiness too. I want to...." she cut her words short.

"Okay, Mom. If you want, I will come," I said gladly.

The thrust of happiness was so intense that I didn't even bother what she left was an incomplete sentence, hiding some secret behind. I somehow managed to tell Abhi this and he reacted with an angry glance. I was happy that finally I was able to meet my love when she was about to start for her hometown. I kept thinking of Neha throughout the journey. How would I greet her? Will I be able to kiss her again? Or will we just be allowed to meet like prisoners within a definite time period. But something is better than nothing. At least god was magnanimous enough to allow us to share this moment, for which she had shed tons of tears. As we reached home, I embraced Mom and greeted her with a soft peck on her forehead. She didn't give me a cheerful response; instead, gave me a fake smile.

"Hey Mom, what happened? Finally, you called me. I knew that you love me so much." We were talking in the kitchen, as it used to be our favourite place for any conversations like that.

"Beta, do you love me?" she asked while gazing deep into my eyes.

"Of course. I love you a lot. That's why I have come here, for your happiness," I smiled and cuddled her.

"Beta, I cannot tell you what she did to me!" Mom said. Her words pricked my eardrums hard.

"What Mom? What has happened now? What did she do?" I was shocked and angry at the same time.

"Beta, yesterday your father was on a tour, leaving me to take care of Neha. Sometimes, I feel my nerves bursting under the pressure. That doesn't mean I am against both of you beta. I am your Mom and I am extremely worried about both of you. In these situations, who is there that I can lean on? I called Mrs Shukla to appease my pain. When we were in the drawing room, she tried to soothe my pain to make me feel better. But it all went awry when Neha snapped in, with such wide open eyes and heavy breaths. Her eyes were fuming in anger and after that she started throwing tantrums at me without a pause. She uttered such bitter words about me and our family that I can't even share with you, my son!"

I felt like collapsing on the floor. I caught hold of the countertop to steady myself. The girl for whom I had come had done a horrific thing. I couldn't believe my ears. "Really, Mom? Tell me in detail what happened. Please Mom....."

"I know, beta. I did not expect this from her either. I ignored her shortcomings just because you love her, beta. She should

understand this. She thinks I am creating problems between you and her. She was so loud in her tone that she really scared the hell out of me!" Mom started crying and I embraced her.

"Why did she do that? Was there any conversation? Any heated argument before that? Did she just enter and start yelling at you? I want to know what all she said Mom, and everything that happened!"

"Beta if you want to know... I will tell you," she added.

"'What do you think of yourself Aunty? Why can't you see us happy? Why do you give us so much pain? I also belong to a reputed family and they have not left me here to entice a boy for myself! Even my family won't be ready for this marriage. I will have to convince them somehow. You think they would be ready for marriage after hearing about your family? About your brother, who eloped with some character-less woman... about uncle's sister, to whom you don't speak... about Dadaji's murder... Why do you just keep blaming my family, Aunty?'"

I felt giddy and asked Mom to stop immediately. My breathing was getting heavier and I immediately left the place. "Sunny! Please don't say anything to her. She has already apologized," Mom yelled after me, but I just marched inside her room in anger. I smashed the door open and she got scared, while sitting on her bed.

"Oh Sunny! Please take me away from here." She immediately looked towards me and stood up to hug me.

"Why did you do this Neha? Why?" I yelled at her with my red angry eyes. She fell back on the bed, gazing at me with questioning eyes. "Everything is finished, Neha. We are done!" I yelled.

"I want to go home, Sunny. I'll die here otherwise. I want to go home to my Mom and Dad. There is nobody for me here."

She fell on her bed as if she was unconscious. I immediately ran towards her.

"Okay, okay. Take long deep breaths, Neha."

She tried doing that, but it didn't help. "Neha...please.... please wake up... I am with you..." I took her hands into mine. She did not speak a word. Her body was numb. I brought water and caressed her back while she sipped it. After a while, she seemed a little relaxed.

"Sunny, I am sorry for whatever I have done. But that was a misunderstanding," she informed me.

"Misunderstanding?" I asked.

"I don't know what Aunty has told you. But, even I don't remember what had happened to me in anger. I went mad when I heard the conversation going on between Mom and Mrs Shukla. They were saying weird things about my family, and that the love acceptance is a mere plan to befool both of us. After all it's a matter of my life, Sunny. I am not a machine. I got completely out of my wits. I am really sorry, Sunny!" she said, leaning against the wall.

"Neha, everybody is going out of control here, giving an excuse of love, care and affection. If these words are so cruel and harmful, then god keep us away from them. But Neha, you've made a blunder this time, and you should realize that. You don't know how hard I am struggling to keep our love alive. Had you realized that, you would have called me. But you have given them a reason this time, to force separation on us. You have left me with no choice but to follow what Mom says. I could take a stand for our relationship had you not made this mistake. You have forced our relationship to end on a bad note," I left the room, slamming the door shut.

A Miracle

Miracles are not mere coincidences; they are a result of your immense emotions.

Kashi Vishwanath Temple

The very next morning, Ashu was fast asleep, unaware of the shock that Sunny was going to throw at him. Suddenly, he flipped around on bed, embracing the pillow between both his legs, making a sensuous sound. After a moment his eyelids appeared to form a thin line of separation to allow some fresh rays of sunlight inside. He impulsively sprang out of bed and rubbed his almost swollen sleep-clogged eyes to clear his hazy vision.

"Oh shit! Not again! Where the hell is he?" he patted his palm over his forehead involuntarily, expressing utmost frustration. He jumped out of bed to look for his escapist friend. He grabbed his phone, only to find a message notification flashing on the locked I-Phone screen. He unlocked it at the speed of lightning and read the message:

Happy Shivratri in advance, my friend, and sorry for not letting you know about my surprise visit... surprise escape, in fact. I know this is the second time that I am leaving you uninformed. I'll explain everything to you later. But all I can say now is, thank you so much for showing the path to this struggling lost traveller. Maybe this time I will make it, fingers crossed!

Ashu gazed at the screen; his expression curious. After pondering over it, a smile lit his face and he murmured,

"He is completely mad yaar..." Ashu said to himself as he replied,

Okay, bro! Plz take care of yourself. I will manage everything here. And do not hesitate to call me if needed. I want you in a single perfect piece this time. Mind you.

As he pressed the send button, his phone rang.

'Pawan Sir Calling.'

"Oh shit! Give me some time god, to at least come up with an excuse." He cleared his throat to overcome his nervousness and picked up.

"Hiii sirr... Good Morning!"

"Hi Ashu! Can you and Akshay make it to the venue by 9:00 a.m. today? We have an important meeting with the HR there," Pawan said, in his moderately authoritative tone.

"Yes sirrr... but ...well... aaaa... I can come," Ashu stuttered.

"Still asleep?" Pawan asked.

"Noo sirrr... I am coming but I am afraid to say that, Akshay can't... as he has... gone...."

"Akshay? Gone? Where?" Pawan asked, frightened.

"Actually sir, last night he got a call from his home and there was bad news..." Ashu was ready with a lie.

"What happened?" Pawan asked in shock.

'Ohh god! What should I say? Can't give wrong facts either,' Ashu pondered and then said, "Sir, actually his *pad-daadi* (great grandmother) passed away."

"Pad-daadi? Oh my god! Was she still alive? I mean, even my daadi is not alive now. So, has he left for home?" Pawan asked, surprised.

"Yes sir! He caught a train that was scheduled to depart in the morning," Ashu replied with a faltering voice.

"Okay. If he has already left, what can we do now? It's not good news for us. He is leading all the juniors and he is the one taking care of so many responsibilities. His absence can't be compensated. Ahhh, let's see how it goes," Pawan took a deep breath.

"I'll try my best, sir. He has explained the tasks to me. So I will manage," Ashu tried to re-assure Pawan.

"Okay. So now, you and Ishita will lead the juniors' crew. I want both of you to work hard day and night for this. We must create a brilliant impression before those organizations. Also, I think there is no need to re-iterate that we have to stand by the coveted legacy of the BHU tag, which companies have associated with us since years. An international seminar is scheduled after two days, wherein the CEOs of top shot companies will be making an appearance, including BHU alumni as well. We have to hit the nail, Ashu. Do you understand how important this is going to be?" Pawan said in one go, as if to reflect the significance of that seminar and emphasize on the consequences of Sunny's uninformed departure.

"Yes sir, I do. Don't you worry. We'll definitely manage," Ashu said, to show confidence this time. Maybe he was anxious about his performance, but he was equally excited to assist Ishita. The next two days were going to be back-breaking for both seniors and juniors. Drafting PPTs, visiting companies, giving presentations, and facing the terrible Delhi traffic. Everyone gathered at night to summarize the day and plan the next one. They were peeping into their laptop screens just like programmed robots. The love between the two mute lovers was getting richer day by day, working together. What Ashu had not been able to do in such a long time was happening now, spending time with Ishita. And Sunny's uninformed escape turned out to be a golden opportunity for fostering the love between them. That night, both Ishita and Ashu were tensed about next day's preparations and they were missing their hero at the same time.

"Hey Ashu, don't you think Sunny is mad?" Ishita asked while playing with the keys of his laptop with her proficient fingers. Ashu gave her an intimidating glance, totally disagreeing with what she was saying to him.

"I mean, he takes his decisions so impulsively and please don't mind me saying, but this way, he is spoiling his life. I know you are his best buddy and you won't admit it, but that's a fact," Ishita said.

"Hmm... Actually, Miss Ishita, my friend listens to his heart and that is something you might call his weakness. But for me, it is his strength. It depends on how he gets affected in a particular situation which decides if it is his strength or weakness. Strength in a way because that makes Sunny, 'The Sunny' for us. He is pure at heart, like a child. And weakness, I think I need not explain... you better know it," Ashu replied staring directly into her eyes.

"Okay. I am sorry if I have hurt your emotions, Ashu. But has he really gone for his great-grandmother's funeral?" she asked. Ashu just glanced at her and kept quiet.

"I got it. No need to explain," she stretched her legs to flex her muscles for comfort. Suddenly, their meditative glance was interrupted by an alert on Ashu's cell.

Open the door.

Ashu flew over Ishita, managing a long jump directly from the bed to the door which was almost five metres away. She was shocked at his sudden reaction and yelled, "Ouchh! Is there a bomb?"

Ashu opened the door and Sunny jumped onto his friend and shouted, "Yey! Yippy!" Ashu jumped in air to embrace him completely, and his legs encircled his waist. Sunny loosened his grip as soon as he realized Ishita was also seated in the room. Ashu's legs slipped down impulsively and he tried to manage his composure. Ishita's shock-stricken face almost froze at this gesture.

"Ahh… I am back guys! Don't worry, Ishita, Ashu is straight. I mean, we both are straight," Sunny said, attempting to cover up what his and Ashu's body language had involuntarily communicated to Ishita. Ashu broke his immobility and said, "Ishita it's… just a friendly gesture… nothing else."

"Okay, I know you guys. Sometimes I wonder why you guys have to… but leave it! You look happy, Sunny. Has your pad-daadi returned?" she said and all three broke into gales of laughter.

"Bhai, now come to the point and tell us what happened. Your excitement is telling me the story of your victory," Ashu questioned him.

"Bhai… There is a lot to tell you," Sunny said with a sigh of relief. "Where should I start from?" he added.

"Ohh! Bhai, from the very start. Please don't test my curiosity. You don't know about the suffering that I had to welcome in your absence. We have to prepare for tomorrows' seminar as well," Ashu snapped in a little irritated tone.

"Oh seminar!" Sunny responded in an uncanny way and took his laptop out of his bag.

"Bhai, what are you doing now? We'll work together later. Let us know about your journey first. Did you meet bhabhi this time?" Ashu asked, moving his hand forward to snatch the laptop away from him.

"One minute Ashu!" Sunny commanded. "Will you both please provide me your valuable inputs on this?" Sunny said, opening one of the PPTs and handing over the laptop to Ashu and Ishita. Both Ashu and Ishita looked puzzled. They looked through it, slide by slide, and their mouths were wide open, gazing that Sunny was already prepared for next day's events. Ishita's jaw dropped seeing this.

"Oh my god! This is wonderful. So enriching it is," Ishita said in a whisper.

"Where have you got this from?" Ashu asked.

"Got this from? What do you guys think? Your Sunny is so mean that he'll leave you alone, to keep struggling amidst such back-breaking tasks, just for the sake of his own benefit? I utilized every spare moment since the day we came here, just to brush up my masterpiece." Sunny winked.

"Brushing up the master piece! You mean this is your masterpiece?" Ashu asked.

"Yes, it is. I have been working on it for the last two months and I have included my research as well. I am pretty confident that it'll be welcomed by companies." Sunny smiled, complementing it with a spirit of confidence and satisfaction. Ashu felt goose bumps on his body to see the spark and dedication in his eyes.

"Ishita, have you seen my mad impulsive friend who is spoiling his life? Yes, this mad boy is my friend," Ashu said emphatically, overwhelmed with emotions and ruffled Sunny's hair with a gentle touch of his palm.

"So guys, do not worry about anything. I'll help you prepare for tomorrow," Sunny said.

"Thanks Sunny. We are proud of you!" Ishita said. Ashu smiled at Sunny. "I'll share that good news with Pawan sir," Ashu picked up his phone.

"I've already informed him that we are done with the PPT," Sunny added.

"'We! You are great, my bro. You always replace 'I' with 'we'! Thanks a lot," Ashu said, patting his back. Ishita was feeling guilty for the misunderstanding that she had about Sunny.

"Okay, please tell us what happened there. Did you meet Neha?" Ishita asked.

The night I shared my story with Ashu, I did not realize that I was reliving my memories, with every minute detail. I actually started living those moments again, as if I had travelled back in time. I couldn't sleep the whole night. I was just tossing around in bed, combating with my maudlin thoughts. I pondered upon what could be done next. How should I proceed further? Will I get my love back or not? Questions shuffled about in my mind like a volleyball game, making me anxious every moment. Sometimes I questioned myself. Should I move on? That day, something happened, which infused a ray of hope in my mind. Ashu mentioned something about his faith and devotion towards Kashi Vishwanath and its significance to him on the day of Shivratri. He said that he was missing the sight of the Vishwanath Temple and the grand aura of that festival in

Banaras. Baba immediately gave me a signal and I took no time in deciphering the clue. Neha's words echoed in my brain that 'Baba will reunite us'. She had once told me, long ago, that, she visited the Kashi Vishwanath Temple every year on Shivratri. Actually this information was lodged deep somewhere inside my subconscious mind, but it suddenly popped up when Ashu mentioned Shivratri. At the same time, the taxi drivers' words kept reverberating in my ears, "This year Shivratri is going to be very special babuji; it is falling on the day of the lunar eclipse."

I recalled the hullaballoo in Banaras, when we were travelling to the railway station to come to Delhi. I recalled the way the city was bathed in the preparations to witness the huge mob of devotees on the eve of Shivratri. I was sure Neha would be visiting the temple this time. The next day was Shivratri, so without wasting a moment, I left for Banaras that night. I felt as if some supernatural positive energy was guiding me, and it had overpowered me to take me closer to Neha. My instinct said that I would get to see her. One reason was that she visited the Vishwanath Temple every year; and secondly, it was going to be special, so she was supposed to come, if not any other year. I struggled in the general bogie for some sixteen hours, but I felt no pain, as my enthusiasm of meeting her had overpowered my mind. Everything happened at the speed of lightning. I don't know what force was responsible for it, but I could feel the universe conspiring in my favour. I reached Banaras and hired an auto to take me to the temple. I was thinking about her each moment. It led to the secretion of endorphins inside my veins. Tripping and stumbling, I reached the threshold of the magnanimous Vishwanath Baba. The area was highly vibrant with a myriad of devotees, accumulating from all around the country. The narrow streets were bustling with small shops. There was a huge crowd that had gathered in the temple premises, and it was getting hard even to spot people out. I had no clue how to find her. Faith in my heart kept me going with the flow, letting god execute his master plan. The energy that was guiding me to fulfill the pursuit of my love kept me moving all the while; even when I did not have a concrete plan. I was not stepping ahead, rather steps were taking me through the narrow streets, leading to the holy cluster of temples. My steps froze automatically at the entrance of the main temple. With each breath, I prayed to meet her. I glanced at every face coming across, unfazed of what people would think about me. My anxiety grew more as time passed, giving me a sense of futility. I approached the revered pious place, following a long queue, but my awkward behaviour was making others suspicious of me.

"Stand straight!" a lady snapped in an authoritative tone and restricted my movement. It was my turn in front of the idol and I bowed down. Tears trickled down my cheeks, to flow on to the base of that holy idol. I felt a sudden push from behind and stumbled onto the floor.

"Oh, sorry brother!" A familiar voice came from behind me. I regained my composure and turned around.

"Rohan! Hey bro! How are you? Been a long time!" I stuttered in surprise and my eyeballs started roaming about impulsively to find my love. I was chatting with him, but my eyes were not fixed on Rohan. Finally, the thirst ended, when Rohan moved forward and those pretty eyes peeped out, for which I was longing since the last two-and-a-half years.

"We should move ahead, Sunny. The queue is too long and we have to take seven rounds!" Rohan said, to which I was completely indifferent, as I was busy witnessing the sight I had been longing for since years.

"Yeah, sure!" I mumbled. She hid behind Rohan and it was getting too difficult for me to rotate my head over and over again. After we completed the rituals, we assembled at a corner. "So, Rohan. Where did you go missing for this long?" I asked him.

"Actually, I was struggling for placements. So, I thought to isolate myself from people. But finally, I cracked it and I have come here to thank Baba. Even my lovely sister Neha had kept a fast for me," Rohan said, visibly filled with gratitude towards her. He placed his hand on her head as a gesture of giving her a blessing. She was standing there quietly and I was not able to decipher her expression, whether she was happy or sad, and that was making me more anxious. I wanted to talk to her, but not a word escaped my mouth. Maybe I was not prepared to listen to the negatives, if any. Our eyes interacted in between, but I was not able to understand what she was trying to communicate.

"That's awesome Rohan. Congratulations! Baba answers everyone's prayer," I said, throwing a glance at her and she passed a momentary smile. Her eyes told me that she understood what I was trying to say to her. By now, I had deep faith in Baba.

"Hmm… And both you brothers are doing great! Hmm… I keep myself updated with both of your whereabouts. After all, your parents' hard work has paid off. Hey, how are they, by the way?" Rohan asked me.

"They are fine," I replied. So many questions were running in my mind, and the answer to all of them was standing right in front of me. But I couldn't find the guts to ask. Should I ask about her marriage? What if the answer turns out to be a yes? I knew, I would not be able to take a yes for that question. Should I ask about her MBA? What if she hadn't got though even now. It was a touchy topic. Finally, I got an idea.

"Rohan, where are you staying?" I asked him, to keep the conversation going, because I wanted to take a step forward. I had not come to know about Rohan's placement scenario. I wanted to take my long lost love-story to the next level.

"Nowhere. We have to catch the train which is scheduled to depart in the evening!" he replied shrugging his shoulders.

"Okay great. Share your number and stay in touch!" I said, while flipping my cell-phone out.

"I changed my number recently. So, I don't even remember it exactly. Give me your number. I will make note of it," Rohan replied. Finally, the trick worked. That's what I wanted to happen, to share my number with Rohan.

"Sure... it is 9... 8... 3... 2... 3... 4... 6... 5... 1...7," I said every digit with clarity, pausing in between, so that she could memorize it. I knew that if she hadn't gotten married till now, she would definitely call me. And we parted after that.

"Oh! So you did not talk to her? Oh my god! What have you done?" Ashu asked.

"Patience!" Sunny said.

"After that, I caught my train to Delhi. I was filled with emotions, surprised to experience the miracle of Baba, and anxious also, as I couldn't talk to her at all. The feelings were inexplicable. Suddenly, I received a message.

Neha- Do you still love me?

My heartbeat broke all the barriers of emotions, as I saw the screen flashing with that question.

Me- I will, till my last breath. And you?

Neha- I will love you even after my last breath.

Tears rolled down my eyes with an overwhelming smile.

Me- It was a long wait, though.

Neha- I had vowed to Shivji today, that I'll break my fast only after I see you. See? He brought you right in front of me. That is my faith in Vishwanath Baba, Sunny; something that I always kept talking about.

Me- I witnessed the miraculous power of your faith today, Neha. There was some force guiding me since the last 24 hours. I ran back from Delhi, in between my Industrial Visit schedule, just to meet you today. I have boarded the train back to Delhi.

The exchange of messages went on, and we, the love birds, kept chirping all the while, giving a new dimension to our love story.

"Fantastic!" Ashu and Isha said in unison. "Finally you talked to bhabhi," Ashu added.

"Yes. That's the good news. Now, let's get back to the presentation. We have to nail it well," Sunny replied.

The industrial visit turned out to be a huge success after Sunny's presentation on the International Seminar Day. Organizations were convinced by the rapport that BHU tried to build before them, and they assured to hit the college on zero-day of the placement season. BHU won the first prize, thanks to the fantastic presentation made by Sunny. Ashu ensured that the prize money remained with Sunny, because he was the mastermind behind that presentation, though they reflected it as team-work.

Love Gets Deeper

September 2012

Sunny began working on every possible aspect of Neha's life to get it back to normal, after whatever had gone wrong in the last two-and-a-half years. He finally convinced her to re-attempt CAT. To appear for her exam, she chose Banaras as the centre.

"Oh wow, great! That is an awesome news....When? When? When?" Sunny asked Neha.

"The 26th of this month...tantadaaaa!"

"Oh my god! I can't believe this. So we are meeting again, after that mute-meeting at the temple. That's great, Neha!"

"Hmm.... And the credit goes to me. You don't know the efforts I had to put in to convince my friends and my mom. I could only convince three of my friends to select Banaras as the exam centre instead of Patna, and that too when I lured them with the grandeur of the Vishwanath temple along with its associated wonder stories till they were eager to visit it."

"Ohho, very smart! Your Vishwanath Baba is miraculous, Neha, I must say!" Sunny replied, praising Neha.

"Okay! Prepare well for the exciting meeting ahead," Sunny ordered.

"Okay sir. I'll buy some sexy dresses... Yay!" Neha was more excited than Sunny about her visit to Banaras.

"Hmm... Good. I have never seen you like that," Sunny said. "And yes, there is a guest house close to the railway station; it's named Paradise. I have booked it."

"Sounds cool. So you'll come there to meet me?" Neha asked.

"Come there? I'll stay with you that night, sweetheart," Sunny spoke with merriment in his voice.

"No... no... no Sunny... Not before marriage! *Na baba na*!" Neha said, worried.

"I am not going to stay in your room, Neha. I have booked one more room for myself in the same guesthouse. So that we can spend the maximum time together," Sunny said.

"That sounds like a good idea! I am coming along with two of my friends. Actually, they make a couple. I think both you boys can occupy one room," Neha trailed off, making some calculations while talking to Sunny.

"That's a great idea! We can shuffle at night for some kisses and hugs," Sunny teased her.

Finally, the day arrived, bringing loads and loads of excitement and nervousness along with it. Sunny stood at the station for three hours, waiting desperately for the train to bring his love along. He recalled those moments when the Bihar train announcements threw up panic attacks. Today, the situation was completely the opposite.

The train announcements struck his ears, and he ran frantically, jostling through the crowd, to reach her bogie, S4.

His heartbeat rose drastically, eyeballs moved hastily in search of Neha among the flood of passengers moving out of the train. He saw her through the window, but the vision was not clear for him in the crowd. She got off the train and he leapt towards her.

"Hi!" Sunny said standing behind her. Her friends passed a confusing smile at him. She turned around and their eyes met.

"Hi... Sunny! How are you?" she smiled coyly. Her expressions clearly showed that she was excited, but she was bordering on shyness.

"So... How was your journey?" Sunny asked her.

She had gained some weight, but it only added to her beauty and glow. Her curves were perfect and well-proportioned, giving her a sexually appealing figure in that tight kurta-legging she was wearing. Her hair was straightened and added beauty to her face. Sunny froze for a moment, embracing her beauty with his eyes.

"Let's move guys," Pooja, her friend broke the hypnotic gaze between them, sensing that Sunny was totally lost in Neha's eyes.

"Ahh... Yes! Let's move! I've already booked a guesthouse for you guys." Sunny said to both of his friends, looking at Neha.

"Oh, that's great," Pooja said. They walked along with Sunny. The lovers kept throwing intermittent gazes at each other. They took a taxi to the guest house. Sunny sat in the front seat, and the three others adjusted themselves in the back seat. Sunny re-adjusted the mirror to peep into it, and gazed at her astounding beauty. She looked unbelievably pretty and gorgeous. Her hair was blowing in the wind. She made futile endeavours to set it behind her ears, and it added to her girlish charm, which took his breath away. He was amazed, wondering if she was the same Neha or some other girl that he was seeing now. They reached the guesthouse after about half an hour. Sunny paid the taxi driver and took all of them inside.

"Hello! We have two rooms booked. 541 and 542. Please check," Sunny said to the receptionist.

"Yes sir! Here are the keys," the receptionist said, and handed over the keys to them with a smile, a mandatory gesture in his profession.

"Which one is ours, Sunny?" Nayan asked.

"541," he smiled handing over the key to him. "And girls, this is yours," he said while unlocking room number 542.

"Thank you so much, Sunny." Pooja smiled.

"The pleasure is all mine, young lady," he showed his gentlemanliness, as he wanted to be nice to Neha's friends.

"You guys freshen up and then we will go out for lunch. I'll take you to the best place in town," Sunny announced. He sat in the other room with Nayan till then.

"So, Pooja is your GF haa! Good. You two make a nice couple," Sunny told him.

"But not as perfect as yours. You both look awesome together," he reciprocated.

"Thanks!" Sunny just winked at him. Both Neha and Pooja entered their room just then.

"What are you guys up to?" Neha asked, while combing her wet hair.

Sunny was getting impatient to embrace her in his arms. He was desperately waiting for the moment that the other couple would leave them alone, to put an end to the years of patience that they both had kept.

"Pooja, let's go for a walk. What do you guys say?" Nayan asked, winking at Sunny.

"Hmm... You guys carry on. We will join you a little later. Let us know if you are going a little farther away."

"Okay! No problem." They said and moved. As they left, Sunny stood up from the bed and locked the door. Neha grabbed him passionately. They hugged each other, moving their hands all over each other's bodies, as if they were trying to capture every touch into their memories. It was purely meditative and was indeed, quite a long hug.

"Oh my love!" Neha said.

"Neha!" Sunny spoke closing his eyes and they were gasping with sensuous breaths.

"I want to be here for the rest of my life, in your arms! Oh god, how long have we waited for this moment, Sunny!" she said caressing his back.

Sunny raised his hands to cup her face in his palms. He looked into her eyes which were filled with the ecstasy of love. He moved his head forward to give her the ambrosia of love through his lips. They shared a passionate kiss that lasted for a long time. They kept shuffling between the upper and lower lips, drowned in the sea of immense emotions. Neha suddenly turned her face to the left, with a shy smile, as she regained her wits.

"What happened, Neha?" Sunny asked.

"Nothing... My heartbeats are exploding, Sunny," she responded shyly.

"Neha, we are meeting by the grace of god. I want to let my soul meet yours," he said and kissed her lips once again. He started kissing all over her face and she got aroused. While kissing, they slowly moved towards the wall, and Sunny grabbed both her hands, kissing all over her neck. They were making involuntary movements, rising automatically with the flow of love. Sunny looked into her eyes, took her in his arms and moved towards the bed. Both of them embraced each other tightly, while lying on the bed. Neha's expressions reflected that her spirit was filled with love and excitement. She surrendered herself, as if she was ready for the infusion of souls. But Sunny confined it to a boundary where he could give solace to her soul, without breaking the pious bond of virginity. He was aware of his responsibilities being her soul-mate. He wanted to yearn for her; first convincing her family, and then giving her the happiness she deserved. Neha lay over his arm with her eyes closed and gave him a comforting smile. She had never smiled that way in the past many years. He removed a curl of her hair that was spread over her face and kissed her forehead. It was a feeling of completeness for both of them.

"I love you, Neha!" he said while giving an overwhelming gaze to her.

"Love you 2… 3… 4… up to infinity, Sunny!" Tears streamed down her nose and she hugged him again. They slipped into a meditative sleep. After some time, Sunny sprang up hastily, and rubbed his sleep-clogged eyes to check the time.

"Neha!" he said, caressing her forehead. She gripped his fingers into hers and raised her hand for a kiss. The beautiful smile on her lips attracted Sunny to kiss them even more and even harder this time.

"Baby, they can come in any time," Sunny whispered while kissing her lips. She immediately opened her eyes as if someone had shaken her out of that dreamy world. She was enjoying those beautiful moments and she felt as if she had already gotten married to him. She opened her eyes and straightened her clothes. She got out of the bed and looked for her bag.

"Sunny, come here!" she said while opening her bag placed at the corner of the room. He moved towards her. She took out a plastic bag and gave it to him.

"Heyyy, this is so beautiful!" Sunny said, taking the shirt out of the packet.

"Only for you, my sweetheart," Neha told him.

"But why such an expensive gift, Neha? You need not spend so lavishly on me," he said, taking the shirt in his hands. He knew that she was not earning much from her computer classes and neither had her father given her enough money. She must have bought it after cutting down on her expenses.

"What expensive? After all, you are my would-be...." she gestured a smile at him.

"Thanks Neha. Thank you so much!" He was overwhelmed.

"Will you just keep staring at it?" she asked while unfolding the shirt.

"Turn around. I am not going to take my shirt off in front of you," Sunny said winking at her.

"Ahem.... I should have brought you trousers then!" She laughed.

"Yes. You look awesome, my dear hubby!" Neha said what Sunny wanted to hear.

"Thanks to you, my smart wife," he said taking her into his arms. Sunny slid his hand inside his pocket and took out something that shocked her. He put a gold chain around her neck.

"Oh Sunny! This is still with you!" she exclaimed in surprise, getting overwhelmed after seeing the same pendant that she had left for him on the day of her departure. Tears of happiness rolled down her eyes, as she took it into her hand, and her eyes noticed that the chain attached to it was made of gold. It was not the same chain that she had given to him.

"Sunny! Is this gold?" She asked quite dramatically, clearly in shock. Sunny just smiled. "Sunny! I am really very happy, but I don't deserve this gold chain... this is too expensive, my love! And I know you must have sacrificed so much for this. You can give me all this after we are wedded, sweetheart. It's really hard for me to accept it at this stage. For me, the feeling that you have given to me by putting our token of love safe, is the most precious gift that one can ever give to me. And no materialistic thing in the world can ever overweigh that. I respect your feelings and I have accepted it, but I would like you to keep it with you. Garland me with it on our first night," she said while taking it off.

"Neha, I bought it with my own money. It's from the prize money that I won in the International Seminar during my industrial visit. Do you know something? I won it just a day after I met you at the Vishwanath Temple. I thought it was a blessing from god for our love. I know you care about me and my family, and I really appreciate that, but I would love to see this chain around your neck. I know it would not be safe for you to keep it at home and I am ready to keep it with me until we get married, but please, for now, please adorn your neck with this Neha, for the time that we are together," Sunny said, tying it around her neck once again. Neha could not say a word.

"And where is my 'part'... my love... have you lost it?" Sunny asked while holding her shoulders tightly.

"Do you really think so? I thought your eyes will first go to the pouch lying in that plastic bag, and after that the shirt will come out," Neha replied.

Sunny immediately grabbed the bag and put his hand inside. To his surprise, it was lying there and they got overwhelmed with emotions, going into another passionate and meditative kiss. After some time, Pooja and Nayan came in, and it seemed that they had had a great time together. In the evening, they all went to Kashi Vishwanath temple on Neha's request. They thanked god for bringing them together and took blessings for their life ahead. They visited the Ganga ghats and enjoyed the view of the setting sun.

"Neha... One thing I must say is that you are very lucky to have such a good boyfriend. He is a full package of what an ideal boyfriend should be like. He'll keep you smiling after your wedding as well," Nayan said, while laughing at one of Sunny's jokes. Neha just smiled.

They treasured every moment of that night together, carving indelible memories, which they could carry along with themselves to bear the pain of separation until marriage hooked them back together for a lifetime.

"Neha, wake up! It's already seven," Sunny said, as he knocked at her door. The bed creaked as she got up to open the door.

"Hi Sunny... Good morning!"

Her voice stretched as she was hovering in a subconscious state. She looked more sensuous in that semi-sleepy state and it seemed like she had gotten drunk the previous night. Sunny moved inside and started kissing her.

"Hey! Pooja is also there...." she murmured. He looked at Pooja who was sleeping with her mouth open. Her body was stretched out like a star fish, covering the major portion of the bed.

"But I don't want to kiss her. This precious gift is only meant for you, baby, who must have struggled the whole night in bed to find space to sleep," he said while trying to kiss her again, as she moved her face away.

"Offoo! She'll wake up," she murmured again, while patting him on his arm and Sunny moved away. "Do it silently," she said and moved to touch his lips. They kept doing that till the creaking sound of the bed broke their state. Pooja had turned her side.

"Uff... We have to get ready. You always ditract me... making me late," she said while turning back towards her bag.

"Okay, baba. Get ready soon. I checked the location of your exam centre and it is quite far away. It will take two hours from here."

"Two hours? Oh my god!" she exclaimed and her hand movements paced up drastically. She brushed her teeth like a robot set on a high-speed mode, leaving Sunny totally surprised.

"Wanna come?" Neha asked, peeping out of the washroom and winking at him. Sunny moved to her and she immediately slammed the door shut.

"Get ready, Sunny!" she yelled from inside.

"I have not brought anything here... I will bathe in the hostel after dropping you at the exam centre," Sunny yelled back. Pooja and Nayan were also ready to head to the exam centre soon after.

"Hey Sunny, how far is the auto stand from here? We have already walked so much," Neha asked.

"Don't worry... we are about to reach," he said. They walked a little further before getting into an autorickshaw.

After a two-hour long ride, they neared their destination.

"Madam, please get down, we have reached," Sunny said and they got off. They headed towards the centre.

"Just a minute... Wait, Neha!" he said suddenly and ran away.

"Where has he gone now? We are getting late!" Pooja said to Neha.

"You go... I'll come," Neha replied.

"Okay, then we will check our roll numbers in the meantime," Nayan said, and both of them started moving.

"Where have you gone, Sunny?" she murmured under her breath, looking for Sunny. As time passed, the lines of stress carved deeper on her face.

"Madam... the exam is about to start. The entrance will be closed soon," the guard at the gate informed her. Suddenly, she saw Sunny running at thundering speed towards her with a scrap of newspaper resting on his palm.

"Here, take this! Give two to them as well. I am sorry, I tried my best and this is all I could find. This place is so barren, you see," he said, trying to gasp for breath and pushing a samosa into her mouth. Moved by this gesture, she whispered, "Why?"

"You haven't had anything since morning and that traffic jam... well, we all were in haste. Now, please... Eat this and go! Best of luck! You'll definitely nail it this time; Shiv ji is with us," he tapped her face with his palm gently, and gestured a slight kiss.

"Thank you so much, my love! I know I will nail it this time, because you are with me," she said, looking at him with her wet eyes, her spirit filled with love and gratitude.

They were reluctant to part. She kept turning around again and again. He smiled and showed a raised thumb to her, gesturing 'good luck'. She was surprised as she felt grateful to god and her fate for blessing her with such a good lover. Sunny was still trying to let it sink in that he had been able to spend a wonderful time with his beloved, after nearly three years. He couldn't believe that he had kissed her after such a long and painful separation. It was like their dream coming true.

Three hours later, Sunny stood at the gate, waiting like the others, for them to come out after the three-hour-long battle. He was impatient to see her face, hovering between the gate and the ground, which was meant to be the waiting place.

"Bhaiya, what happened? There is still half-an-hour left," the guard said, noticing his impatience. He just nodded in response. His eyes frantically scanned the faces to find the one who would accelerate his heartbeats. Many students came out. He couldn't find her or the other couple. Soon, there weren't any more coming out.

"Bhaiya! Why have the students stopped coming out?" Sunny asked the guard.

"They are coming in slots, according to their exam timings. Wait! She'll come," he said and smiled. Again, a bunch of students arrived. After a while, he recognized his love, stepping out and walking slowly. She also noticed him from a distance, and waved at him.

"Happy now?" the guard asked, with a supportive smile. Sunny nodded.

"How did your exam go, darling?" Sunny asked, cuddling her shoulders.

"Good, of course! Your wishes were with me." Neha smiled. Sunny and Neha tried to control their emotions as the time was approaching to separate.

Nayan and Pooja also looked happy with their exam. After chit-chatting a bit, they left for the railway station, as they had to catch a train back.

"Why are you smiling Sunny?" Neha asked, getting emotional, clutching his hand firmly. They were now sitting on a bench on the platform, waiting for the train. She had lost her joy by then. It was getting tougher for them to separate. Re-separate, to be precise.

"Did you hear this announcement, Neha? Whenever I entered the station, I tried to listen to the announcements about trains going to and coming from Bihar. I used to run after them madly, from one platform to another, jostling through the packed crowd, stumbling, falling and jumping, all in the hope that maybe one day, just one day, I would see your face among those many faces in the crowd," he said, turning towards her. His voice was getting heavier. Neha got more emotional and her grip tightened involuntarily, as if her hands did not want to leave his at any cost. She was shocked to know how hard Sunny had struggled to keep his love-story alive and to wait for her. Suddenly, she felt something which made her uncomfortable. She exhibited an expression of unease, which Sunny noticed.

"What happened, Neha? Stomach pain?" Sunny asked.

"It was painful since the morning. I think I am having my periods. Can you see if there is a stain?" she said, standing up.

"No. There isn't one. Oh wait... A little drop, I think," he replied, taking care not to appear awkward in public to be seen staring at her.

"Shit! I was scared about this. I should have worn a pad in the morning," she said, while looking frantically for one in her bag.

"The ladies' washroom is on that side. We can go there. Don't panic, we still have fifteen minutes for the train to start, and we can easily make it back by then," he said.

They marched to the washroom and Neha entered inside. She turned around once; Sunny gave her a gentle smile as if to say that everything would be fine now that he was there. This was the first time Sunny had encountered such a situation with a girl. It was a little strange for him to see that, but at the same time, it gave him a special feeling of 'being a husband'. It did give him a sense of belonging as the woman of his life was sharing something that bore utmost importance to her, with him. A few minutes passed, making him tense. He kept gazing at the faces of women walking out of the ladies' washroom and they gave him intimidating looks.

"Oh bhai! This is the ladies' washroom! Yours is on that side!" one of the ladies growled at him from inside.

"Sorry! Actually, I am waiting for someone. Can you please...? Okay, forget it!" Sunny tried to appease the awkwardness in the situation.

"If you want to wait, sit there!" she snapped and marched back inside. The announcement announcing the train's departure escalated his worry, but he could do nothing about it. His heartbeat turned normal as he saw her coming out of the washroom in a different attire. She had changed from her jeans and top to a kurta and leggings.

"Run fast!" Sunny said to her.

"It was completely packed and filthy. I puked as well. Let's run now," she said. They ran towards the train, holding hands.

"Neha!" Nayan yelled from a distance and waved at them. They looked at him and sped up. The train hooted and Nayan gestured to them to step inside the nearest bogie.

"Come Neha!" Sunny immediately pulled her through the mob, and lifted her slightly to push her inside the door. The train started, taking her away from him, slowly. She stood at the door and he ran along with the train as far as he could. Despite his instructions, she couldn't control the explosion of her tears. She flailed her hand outside, yearning to grab his. She was astonished and touched by the way Sunny ran along with the train and waved. She could imagine how he must have run behind the trains from Bihar just to find her.

"Am I so special god, that you have blessed me with such a lover?" She thought and gestured to him to stop. The train moved on, taking her love away from her, once again. He wore his aviator glasses just to hide his tears and left the station with heavy steps.

The Conspiracy Revealed

Sunny went back to his hostel and got occupied with his studies. Placements were to take place the following week. All night long, both Sunny and Ashu were busy brushing up on their concepts and preparing for interviews. Sunny called Neha the next morning to ensure if she had reached home safe, but the call went unanswered. For the next five days, they were painstakingly busy. They were occupied, attending pre-placement talks, presentations and running through the organizations' memoranda, building their job profiles, discussing packages offered, taking up written tests, a series of HR interviews and what not! Sunny cracked the first company that hit the campus, Infosys, and had the offer of a good job role from them. Ashu worked hard and bagged a job offer from IDBI Bank. It was fantastic for Sunny, as his dreams were finally being realized. He called his father to tell them about his accomplishments, and to seek their blessings. Sunny's mother jumped with joy when she learned that Sunny had carved his niche. She promised him that she would throw a grand party for all the relatives at Sharma Villa, way better than what she did when Sunny had secured admission in BHU. It was time for Sunny to tell the love of his life about his success story and share the moment for which they had put their love-life on halt.

In the bustle that the placements brought along, Sunny had not been able to call Neha in the last six days. It was at the Banaras station when he talked to her last, before she left for Munger. He called her immediately to share the good news with her.

"Please receive the call, Neha. Where are you?" He yelled out loud, walking up and down in his room. The phone kept ringing but the answer that Sunny got was, 'The person you are trying to reach is not responding. Please try again, later.'

'Oh god! Please help me. She did not talk to me after starting from Banaras. What happened to her? She did not even tell me that she had reached safely! No message, nothing!' he thought. He jumped on his bed suddenly, and opened his laptop to browse the train status.

"IRCTC... Where is the column... Which train... Train... Yeah this one... Status..." He took deep breaths while surfing anxiously. "Google... Tell me... Has there been any mishap recently? No... No... No... Six days ago... Thank god! Where the hell is she, then? She would never do this! She would at least leave a message saying she has reached safely."

Sunny was unable to be at ease. More than the excitement of meeting Neha or sharing his placements news, it was her whereabouts that were keeping him worried. Suddenly, his phone beeped, signalling that a message had come.

Sorry Sunny... Couldn't reply! Papa's health is extremely bad. My phone will be with Rohan bhaiya. Can't say anything more than that. Try not to contact. Will be better for both of us. I will call you whenever possible for me. I hope you understand.

That message left him clueless. At least regular communication would have pacified the situation to some extent, but even that door was closed by Neha.

December 2012

Sunny was on his way back home, with mixed emotions about his bright career and the anxiety of facing the toughest challenges in life. When it was time for him to talk to family about marriage, Sunny was left uncertain. He had thought earlier, that it would be easier once he got his career in place, but as time passed, the reasons for their separation only worsened. The excitement of his placement was overpowered by the dreaded apprehensions of permanent separation. 'How should I start? How will I convey this to Mom and Dad? How will I convince her family?' He kept rehearsing his dialogues. He moved to the upper berth in the train and fell asleep, after hours of pondering.

"Beta! Dehradun has arrived," a soft voice penetrated his ears, but didn't reach the threshold to wake him up.

"Mr Consultant from Infosys!" A heavy voice pricked his ear drums, which was impossible to ignore. He sprang up frantically.

"Ohh my god! Mom? Dad? Am I in Dehradun?" he asked, rubbing his sleep-filled eyes.

"No Beta... We are in Banaras!" His father mocked. All three of them laughed and made their way towards the parking lot after Sunny got off, jostling through the crowd all along. Sunny and his mother waited as his father went to get the car. "So, Beta! How was the journey?" Mom asked with a broad smile.

"It was okay. When did you arrive?" Sunny asked her.

"Beta, we have been here for the last three hours, waiting for my *jigar ka tukda*!" She pulled his cheek.

"Consultant saab... The car is ready with the driver. Please get in," Mr Sharma said, stopping the car in front of them. His mother got on in front, and Sunny sat in the backseat with his bulky bag.

"I have made rajma chawal for my son!" she said emphatically, to show her affection for Sunny.

"That's great. Mom, I love you so much!" Sunny exclaimed.

"I think you should make frequent trips home, Sunny. At least I will be benefitted by your arrival. Otherwise I am given only regular dal and chapatti meals!" Papa said in between, with his usual sense of humour to trigger laughter.

"You speak as if I never take care of your choices, Sharma ji," she said, frowning. The happiness on his parents' faces made him reluctant to rake up old wounds. He was perplexed and decided to wait for an opportune moment to speak about marriage. They reached home and sat down for lunch. There was a hum of the usual discussions that happens between father and son on the dining table.

"Sunny, when do you join?" Papa asked, mixing rajma gravy in rice.

"In June, Dad."

"Okay, great! Finally, the time has arrived that you taste the ripened fruits of your endeavours. We are really proud of you, my son!" he said. "Abhi has also bagged the scholarship and he is moving to US soon," Papa added while chewing.

"Hmm Papa, I know that," Sunny nodded.

"We are free from our responsibilities now, Rekha! Thank god!" Papa said with a sense of satisfaction.

"No. There is still one left," Mom pricked his satiating expression, moving out of the kitchen, taking the rajma curry along. "Their weddings," she said, as she served them both some more rajma.

"So many friends of mine referring good girls for them. I'll find the best angels for my smart sons."

Sunny's stomach knotted tightly and he was unable to swallow a morsel.

"Mom, please, give me some water," he said, feeling uncomfortable at her words.

He drank water and added, "Okay, Mom. I am done. I am tired now. Will rest for while." He stood up suddenly, pushing his chair back, and went to his room. The ambience inside the house was killing him from within. The aroma, the position of the furniture, the hangings and everything else – they all made him recall the past. He was disturbed at the thought of his marriage that his mother had proposed. She looked happy about it and he was in no mood to shatter her happiness. He was numb at the thought of marrying any girl but Neha. On the other hand, Neha had already left him alone because of her father's deteriorating health. He was clueless and blank about what to do.

'Dear god! Give me a way out. What should I do now? I don't want my family to land into a traumatic situation again!' he thought and sobbed, covering his face with a pillow. With all that worry and pressure, Sunny's health slowly started deteriorating. He started to escape all conversations with his mother, which was easily noticed by his parents.

"Beta... what has happened to you? You have been looking sad since you arrived!" his mother asked.

"I am okay, Mom! I just feel a little tired these days," Sunny tried his best to make an excuse.

"Why Beta? What happened? I have noticed this change in you for the last five days. Every day, you feel tired. Is everything fine? Tell me, what is wrong? How can I be happy if my son is not happy? Please beta, tell me. What happened to you? You should be happy that you have got a lucrative job, and instead, you are gloomy. That's such a surprise to both of us!" Mom said sitting on his bed.

"Nothing, Mom. I am okay," Sunny said avoiding eye-contact with his mother. He covered his face with the sheet and pretended to have fallen asleep. That night, his mother expressed her concern about his behaviour to his father. They thought about the possibilities, but were afraid to consider what their heart was envisaging. They just wanted to rule out all the negative options deliberately. They didn't want their mind to synchronize with what their hearts were whispering to them secretly.

"Do you really think it is possible?" she asked Sunny's father his view on the matter.

"Maybe. No, no, no... It's been over three years now. It's not possible." He took a deep breath, trying to take in more oxygen to soothe his heartbeat.

"You are right. This cannot be the case. He knows that." His mother did not even want to think about it.

"But... what if this is true?" his father uttered in concern.

"Then this time I'll definitely listen to my heart. I'll go with my son. I cannot see him die every day," she said. They smiled, looking at each other.

"But it's your duty to find out what is there in his heart," he said, pulling the blanket to cover himself, to which she just smiled in agreement.

All of Sunny's mother's efforts in making him speak were in vain. It disturbed his parents and they finally decided to consult their family doctor. He told them that it was a clear case of hypertension.

His mother had made a firm decision to talk to him frankly and tell him something she always avoided sharing in order to safeguard the mom-son relationship, something that she avoided in apprehension of losing her beloved son. But it was high time now. She made up her mind to turn her heart into stone and tell her son the truth, irrespective of the consequences that may follow. She firmly decided that she would tell him the truth as soon as she found the right opportunity.

He again had that recurring nightmare and he yelled in sleep, "Mom!"

"What happened?" His mother came running to his room with a terrified look. He realized that it was only a nightmare. The next moment, Sunny lay on his bed in a coiled position. His eyelids turned dry as they were deprived of tears. "Nothing, Mom!" he said. His mother moved inside the room slowly. She walked like there were fetters on her legs. Her face turned pale thinking of the consequences. Sunny sat upright on the bed, making space for her. When he looked at her, a feeling of guilt took over his heart.

"Beta! Are you okay?" she asked.

"Yes, Mom. I am fine," Sunny said, avoiding eye contact.

"Beta, I want to talk to you. Please look at me," she said, requesting him in a very polite tone, which was impossible for Sunny to ignore.

"Hmm. Tell me, Mom." Sunny looked at her. He was apprehensive about discussing anything. He was afraid that his tongue would slip.

"Beta, tell me your problem. I am your mother and I can see that you are in pain. Please do not hide anything from me. I love you, my son, and I promise I'll help you sort out the matter," she said with a firm glance to take him into confidence. It seemed to him as if she had already read his mind.

"Mom, I don't know what's happening, but nothing excites me nowadays. I feel lethargic all the time. I don't feel like doing anything. I have been blessed with so many things, Ma – my placements, my friends, my outstanding profile, lucrative job, fantastic academic results – but I feel a complete vacuum inside me, as if someone has sucked all the positivity out of me and replaced it with deep pain. What should I do, Mom? It's getting unbearable now."

"Neha?" Mom spoke in between, leaving him stunned. He tried to swallow the lump forming in his throat. "Just say yes or no, beta. No need to worry about me. I know you love me a lot, but it's time to get things cleared. It's impacting your health now and I cannot take it anymore. I have seen your mood swings, whenever we have talked about your marriage. I have seen you staring at her room with teary eyes. I know every moment she spent here is trapped in this house and it makes you uncomfortable on every visit you make. I think about changing our house sometimes, but then I am forced to drop that idea, thinking about your father's attachment to this place. He has put in his sweat and blood day and night, building the foundations of this house. I was wrong Sunny, I thought things would change with time, that maybe you would move on, but...." she took a deep breath and Sunny listened to her silently. "But now, I can't see your pain, Sunny. I know you are an ideal son and you are suffering a only because of me. But I am not an ideal mother, I guess. I betrayed your feelings. You will have to agree Sunny, that I did all this because I love you and I care for you!" tears rolled down her eyes. Sunny immediately embraced her.

"I know you did everything for my bright future. Please don't cry. Otherwise, I'll also cry, Ma."

"Beta, I know you are sensitive about me. You have a heart of gold. You are killing yourself because of me. I did not even understand your emotions. I was the one..." she said breaking into tears.

"You were the one... What Ma?" Sunny asked, confused.

"I was the one who planned the cheap plot to throw a true girl out of your life, beta, but there was no way out, Sunny!" she added, crying earnestly this time.

"What?" Sunny was astonished.

"Please forgive me, my son. I did all this only for your future," she confessed.

"For my future?" Sunny's voice turned harsh.

"Yes." She looked up into his eyes and said earnestly, "Actually, there is a secret that I did not confide in anyone. Sunny, she had some hormonal problems and I took her to a gynaecologist for the same reason," she said in a heavy voice. Sunny kept on listening to her without any movement in his body. "Beta, the doctor said that she had some severe hormonal problem and maybe because of that she could never become a mother. That's why, I could not imagine her as your bride as I was not able to accept the fact that my daughter-in-law could possibly never conceive. Tell me, Sunny, how can a mother accept such a girl who cannot continue the family's lineage? I was already worried about your career. I always wanted you to avoid any emotional indulgence with her. Above all, this fact shattered me. I loved her a lot, and everybody knows that. But I couldn't control myself after I learnt about your attachment with her. The more she would talk to you, my fear would aggravate and I wondered why she was deliberately cajoling you when I didn't want her to be close to you! I was overpowered by my motherly emotions and I did not want to spoil your future. I couldn't bear the burden of everything that happened just because I brought her home. Both of you were drowned in the ocean of love, and that too, to such an extent that only a powerful thrust could bring you back, Sunny... and... we planned... that..."

"We?" Sunny's eyes got red by now.

"Beta, I am sorry! I can't hide it anymore. I want to speak my mind today and face the consequences of bringing the truth to the table. Mrs Shukla urged me to do all that when she saw me crying. That day, Neha got stuck in a misunderstanding. She heard Mrs Shukla talking to me. Beta, I swear I really accepted your relationship happily. Mrs Shukla suggested that everything would be fine once Neha moves out of the house. She told me that I should demand total isolation in return to accepting your relationship and all this was heard by the poor girl. She was hurt and shattered. She snapped into the room and uttered those bitter words, which were not as bitter as I had told you, Sunny. The moment she moved out, Mrs Shukla told me to use her rude behaviour against her and scale up my depression. I swear Sunny, I was so broken from inside that I was trapped by her words. I lost my senses completely. I am really ashamed of all that, Sunny. I don't want you to go into depression because of me. Please don't worry about me! Those fits were... contrived... They were just fake, Sunny. And I may accept her for you, but please be happy. I want nothing beyond that... I may!" Mom hugged him to stir life in his numb body. He jolted her back.

"Accept for me? What do you mean by that, Mom...? 'Maybe this'... 'maybe that'... Your 'maybe' has spoiled the life of a poor girl. Have you ever put yourself in her shoes? Even if she had any such problem, Mom, then she deserved much more care and love rather than a conspiracy planned against her for permanent rejection. You are also a woman, Mom. Have you ever thought about it even once, what she would have felt when she was warned not to contact a person whom she had already devoted her heart to? She had refused our relationship the day she saw you unhappy, but it was you who gave encouragement to her emotions again, to revamp her shattered dream-world. She also has a heart, Mom…" his voice stuttered as his lips started shaking. His Mom was thoroughly ashamed of her misdeeds.

Sunny continued, "She is not like today's flirtatious, chirpy girls, who would bet on the list of their boyfriends. She's such a pure and pious heart, Mom, and whoever she loves, she would love him till the end. You have ruined our lives, Ma. I have been dying every moment for the last three years. My health has been badly affected because of all this. Is this the future you dreamt for me? What's the rationality behind killing our present just to save our future? Now, my emotions and respect have grown more for her. I should not have blindly trusted you, Ma. But what else would I have done? You are my Mom, right? It's not just a three-letter-word, but the most respectable and coveted title for a woman, who represents an epitome of love. You disrespected that status, Ma, and I am ashamed that I yelled at Neha for the plot that you and Shukla Aunty planned against her!"

Sunny jolted up from the bed and moved out, leaving his Mom to repent for her deeds. The veracity of that black day came as a shock to him. He broke down again. For the first time in his life, he had shown a contemptuous demeanour towards his mom. After venting his pain for hours in a solitary corner of his room, he gave a sudden glance to the droplets on the floor.

They seemed exactly the same as they did some years ago. But they were for a different cause now. Yes, they were different, at least in some respect. That day, they were flowing because of Mom's troublesome condition, while today, knowing the fact that it was nothing but just a lie. Isn't that an irony of life? Is it not a much better condition? Thoughts crawled inside his mind. He was wondering whether to moan over it or to accept the positivity lurking behind those circumstances. Now, his head lightened from the burden of guilt and remorse. The biggest change was that his Mom was ready for her acceptance.

'When everything seems to be on track, why not to start a new story where only love finds a place?' he thought.

The next day, in the afternoon, he went to the living room where his Mom was seated on the sofa, chopping vegetables. Sunny moved closer to her. "Mom!" She seemed lost in thought. "Mom!" he spoke a little louder this time, without being harsh. She came out of that frozen state and her face turned impulsively towards him.

"Yes, beta?" she looked at him politely.

"Mom, I am sorry for whatever I said. Please forgive me. I love you, Mom! I want to forget everything and want to start a new life!" he said and embraced her.

"No beta. Please don't feel sorry. I don't deserve your sorry. I know there is no way in which I can make up for the loss that you have suffered. And there is no apology in the world that can wash off my shameful deed. But still, I am really very sorry beta... From the bottom of my heart... I feel sorry!" she said amidst sobs.

"No, Mom forget everything! I love you, Mom," he said and hugged her. "Mom?"

"Yes, Beta?"

"Your lap is the safest place in this world, Mom. I want to sleep in solace, Ma. Let me sleep in your lap," he said.

"Come, my son," she moved to coil her legs where all his worries would evaporate. Sunny stooped on her lap and she started caressing his hair.

"Mom, do you remember? In my childhood, whenever I felt bad about something, you took me into your lap and caressed my hair in the same way? Then, you would keep telling me motivational stories and would make me learn the toughest lessons of life. I am feeling the same today."

"Hmm... Beta, how I can forget that? For some time, I was lost somewhere. But I have come back now," she said overwhelmed.

An Irreparable Sacrifice

Sunny did not receive any call from Neha, and it was aggravating his fear. The only good thing that happened was that he had got his mom back and she had accepted their relationship happily. She wanted Neha to become her daughter-in-law. He cursed his destiny for taking Neha away from him, when his Mom was with him. Sunny was surfing the internet and suddenly stumbled upon a link that read 'CAT Results'. The CAT results had been released. "CAT results out. Oh man!" he said, and began surfing, more frantically. His heartbeat rose and he started looking for Neha's CAT registration number.

"Please, god! She should nail it this time, please, please, please," he murmured.

"Thank god! I got the registration number. Here, fast, fast! This bloody server! please... Neha Kumari! 96 percentile. Yoohooo! You nailed it, Neha! You nailed it!" he yelled in excitement. "Thank you so much, god. At least, something positive happened in her life," he joined his hands in reverence to pay his gratitude and his eyes grew moist.

He felt as if he had himself gotten into IIMs. He was dying to share the happy news with Neha that their love had survived all the obstacles on its path. He was dying to tell her that their pure love had not become a hurdle in their dreams. Rather, it had provided strength to fulfill them. It had been a month now that she had started from Banaras and his patience was crossing its limit. After hours of pondering and fluctuations of thoughts, he decided to call Rohan, assuming that it would be better to ask his whereabouts. After a long time, the call was answered. He waited for a moment to identify the voice at the other end.

"Hello!"

"Hello!" Sunny said. "Uh... Hi! Rohan! How are you?" he added.

"Ohh! Hi Sunny...I am okay... What about you?" Rohan asked.

"Nothing! Just thought of talking to you. How is everyone at home?" Sunny asked.

"Yaar, Papa is not keeping well these days. We are in Delhi, at AIIMS right now!" Rohan said.

"Oh! I am so sorry to hear about it. How can I help?" Sunny said.

"Thanks, Bhai. It's okay. I will ask if needed," Rohan said, gratefully.

'How should I ask about Neha?' Sunny thought. "So, are you alone there? Or is Aunty with you?" Sunny asked.

"Mom is here. Neha is at bua's place. She was here for a couple of days, but I only took the decision to send her there as she was spoiling her health. She's so emotional, you know?" Rohan said.

"Hmm right! You took the right decision. Take care and do let me know if anything is needed!"

"Sure. Thanks a lot. Really felt good that you called me!" Sunny bade him goodbye and hung up.

'That's why she couldn't call me. What should I do now? It's very tough to wait for circumstances to get back to normal, sitting here doing nothing. What can a person do when the life of his loved one is at stake? The same thing happened to us three years ago, but that was at my end, though I was not aware of the truth at that time. Is it a re-separation? No, god. Not this time! Please, save us.' Sunny thought about her plight and was frightened, assuming it to be a separation again. Sunny went to college to complete his final semester. His days passed by in uncertainty. He landed on the same jagged solitary path where he had been crawling for the last three years. The only difference was that this time, the memories were vivid, and caused excruciating pain. He pondered over it day and night.

'Why did god reunite us in the first place, if the ending was supposed to be so bad? Why did god give us a chance to re-weave beautiful dreams, when he did not lay the plan of letting both of us unite?' he thought.

Wherever he went, he carried the bundle of memories which isolated him from his surroundings. He waded into the ocean of reveries which sometimes made him laugh, while sometimes cry. 'I am sorry for being selfish, god I should have prayed for her father's health. I am so sorry. All I want is happiness in her life... all I wish... that smile to stay on her lips forever... and that smile, never to fade away... please god....please...'

He took a deep breath and said to himself, "I am ready for it, god! I am ready for parting forever if that means her happiness." He stood with his puffed lungs and closed eyes for a few moments. He suddenly stumbled upon a stone, but then he managed his composure. A few more days passed just like that, but nothing made Sunny's condition better. He did not get any call from Neha. All he could do was just pray.

Suddenly, his phone rang

"Hello, Papa!" he tried making his voice normal and maintaining his composure.

"Hello beta. How are you? And how are your semester exams going?"

"Fine! Now the semester has ended and I will be back in Dehradun in a couple of days."

"Beta, actually... uhh..." his father fumbled.

"What happened, Papa? Is everything alright? You sound worried...Where is Mom?" Sunny asked him.

"Yes beta. Actually... Nothing serious as such... You know about Rohan's father and his health?" he said, swallowing a lump in his throat.

"Yes. What happened?" Sunny's voice suggested that he suspected a mishap.

"Beta, we are here to see him. And he's out of danger now. We want you to come and visit him," he told Sunny.

"What? I mean, are you at the hospital?" Sunny asked loudly.

"Yes. We reached here as soon as we came to know. After all, Rohan is also like our son. We thought of paying a visit. Pack your bags and catch the first flight tomorrow. We'll discuss everything later, Sunny," his father broke the news to him.

"Okay Papa! But what made..." Sunny fumbled, as he was unable to find words.

"Nothing, beta. Just come. Nothing negative, just that your Mom wants to see you."

"Okay, sure. Where is Mom?" Sunny was excited realizing that his Mom had sorted out everything.

"Ahh! Beta, uhh...your mother is busy talking to Rohan's mother, she will not be able to talk to you now," Sunny's father replied.

"Ohh yeah, yeah Papa. No problem. I will come soon," Sunny said and hung up. "Yoohoo!" he just yelled in excitement. He was on cloud nine.

'Thank god! Thank you, Mom and Dad. I love you! Love you! Love you! I know you have done everything for me, Mom. Just to get my love back, you have gone there.... Yes! Yes! You have fulfilled your promise, Ma. I can't believe that my parents are with them, helping them in their toughest phase.' He ran out to exude his happiness.

He packed his bag and got ready in no time. He asked about the next flight and got tickets for the same day itself. He could not wait even for a day. He kept an eye on the clock, imagining the scene there. It was after a long time that he could think of something positive – his wedding, his honeymoon and what not! Finally, the time had arrived and he had reached the airport to catch his flight. The station announcements had taken him away from Neha, but the one at the airport today was taking him closer to her. He could not even afford to stay calm for the hours he had to spend in the flight, however few they were. But that was the bare minimum he had to spend to reach her. Finally, they took off and landed at the Delhi airport. He took a taxi to the hospital, not bothering about the fare they charged. He was dying to see his mother with Neha and her family. He had been waiting for this moment for years, when his mother would embrace Neha as her daughter-in-law and this was a moment that he was to witness today. His heart was enthralled with love that his Mom had showered on him by keeping up the promise to get her son's happiness back. He reached the ICU and called his father.

"Papa... I have reached! Where are you all? Where is Rohan's dad?" he asked, while his eyes were frantically looking all around, to look for anyone whom he could recognize.

"I am coming outside, beta, in a moment!" Sunny's father said.

"Papa, bring Mom along. I am dying to see her. After all, she has come here only for me," Sunny said, excitedly. His father came out and embraced Sunny, who reciprocated the same warmth to his dad, but his eyes were looking for his Mom. "Where is Mom? She did not come?" Sunny was curious. More than Neha, it was his Mom whom he wanted to see.

"She is inside, come," Papa said, gesturing. He moved inside, envisaging a surprise. He thought his Mom was sitting beside Neha, giving her a motherly touch and bestowing upon her tender love. The thought filled him with positivity. His steps were energetic and he rushed to take his Mom in his arms. Sunny walked fast and his father found it difficult to keep pace.

"Beta, left, not right! Come with me," his father called out.

"Okay Papa!" he kept moving at his own pace. Finally, he stopped at the ICU, hoping for his mother to greet him and hug him tight.

As he moved inside, he was shocked to see Neha and her mother sitting on the bench, but his own Mom was missing. He was sceptical about the whole situation. Nobody was telling him anything. Neither his father, nor Neha had said a word. What he was witnessing now was contrary to what he had expected. His father finally reached him and they moved ahead. He offered an inquisitive glance to his father, trying to find truth in his eyes. He was frightened that something had happened to his mother and it scared him no end. They moved forward and Rohan paced towards them.

"Hi Sunny!" Rohan greeted him with a smile, but nothing could appease Sunny's trauma. He sensed something was wrong, but no one said anything. He could see everyone except for his mother, and his father's mysterious smile made him even more curious to know the truth.

"Where is Mom, Rohan?" he asked. His voice broke this time, as he was just about to cry.

"She is fine, beta!" Papa replied.

"Where is she, Papa? I want to know. Where is Maa? Tell me, I want to know. I can sense something has happened to her!" he said, nearly bursting into tears this time. He ran towards the ICU and began looking for her as his father had pointed towards it. He shook and trembled, finding that his Mom was not well. Tears were flowing, his body was shivering. His heart was beating fast and he was not able to accept what destiny was trying to point towards. His brimming eyes kept wavering through the glass pane of the ICU to find her. Neha walked up to him and rested her hand on his shoulder to placate him, but to no avail. All her efforts went in vain. What she saw in his eyes was nothing but his inquisitiveness to know what had happened to his mother and why was she put in the ICU. He did not know that the excitement with which he had started from Banaras would turn into utter disappointment after reaching Delhi. Even Neha was not an answer to all the questions that were lingering in Sunny's eyes at that point of time. His eyes stopped suddenly when he saw his mother lying on one of the beds of the ICU. He didn't even care about Neha. He was shaken to see his mother lying inside the ICU, clearly not in her senses.

"What has happened to Mom, Papa? Tell me now!" he yelled, bursting into tears.

"Beta, nothing! She is fine!" he replied.

"Rohan's father was very serious, Sunny," he added.

"Oh! Has she given blood?" he asked. His father was silent. Suddenly, the team of doctors passed by, and one of them came to Sunny's father and spoke to him.

"Your wife is a virtuous soul, Mr Sharma. What she has done today, believe me, no one does even for one's own blood. She has given a powerful message to all of us. Humanity is not dead yet. We are proud to have done a great deed and perform such a crucial surgery," he said, placing his hand around Mr Sharma's shoulder.

"What did she do, Papa? What's happening here? Is anybody going to tell me? Why isn't anyone telling me the truth?" he asked, nearly turning mad at these words from the doctors.

"Beta, your mother saved Neha's father's life by donating one of her kidneys. His father did not have much time to survive as both his kidneys had stopped functioning," Mr Sharma said.

"Kidney? What? Oh my god!" He fell on his knees, totally broken. Sunny began crying as he listened to what the doctors said. He fell on the floor, partly unconscious, and cried his heart out yelling "Mom!" at the top of his voice. He felt that he had lost something really significant. He felt as if destiny had snatched away something too crucial from him, leaving him handicapped.

"Beta, please control yourself! She is fine! This is the ICU, beta!" Sunny's father tried to grab him and make him come back to his senses.

"I want to see my Mom. I want to see her, Papa. Take me inside, please?" He stood up and ran to the huge doors of the ICU, but was stopped by his father.

"I would have given my kidney Papa, if it was that urgent. Why did you do that, Mom? Why did you let her do that, Papa? I could have done it. Why did you allow her?" he cried incessantly.

"Pease calm down, Sunny!" Mr Sharma and Rohan pulled him up and made him sit comfortably on the sofa nearby. Rohan brought a glass of water and consoled him, patting his shoulder and his back.

"Beta! She is perfectly fine. Nobody forced her, Sunny! She wanted to do this. She is fine, trust me. Rohan's father's life is saved too. Look at Neha, and her mother! They have been suffering for the past four months, beta. Your mother has relieved them of their suffering. Your mother has done a great deed, Sunny. She has not just saved Neha's father's life, but she has also infused life in many other hearts as well. She is fine. You can meet her after an hour or so. Relax for now. I knew that you will be broken knowing about this. That is why I did not break that news to you over phone," his father said, as Sunny's head rested on his chest.

"It's okay. Beta, relax. You should be proud of your mother. Take deep breaths. Everything is going to be fine," his father said, caressing his back lovingly.

Sunny stood up to move to the ICU. Neha supported him with Rohan. She kept speaking to him while walking along.

"Sunny, I can understand your pain, but she has done it on her own will. My mom offered her kidney to papa, but she couldn't qualify the medical test. Aunty did not let me or Rohan bhaiya take the step. Believe me, Sunny, she took this decision herself. She said that, 'There is no bigger worship than saving a life, even if it means donating an organ.' She is magnanimous, Sunny. Aunty is great. I have no words to express the respect I have for her. Do not ruin her sacrifice this way, by simply crying. What she deserves is far beyond what you and I can do together," Neha said. Sunny walked slowly, as if his legs had been burdened.

His expressions were frozen when he said, "It's not just any sacrifice, Neha... it's an irreparable sacrifice."

"Does Abhi know about it, Papa?" he asked his father.

Papa shook his head and added, "Don't worry, he is returning from the US after two weeks. Everything will be fine by then and I will inform him!" he said, with a consoling glance. Sunny moved inside to see her Mom with his father and Neha. He lost composure when he saw his mother surrounded by medical instruments and needles piercing her skin. His heart cried like never before. She saw Sunny from the small parting of her eyes. She recognized him immediately and twitched one side of her lips, trying to smile. She showed some movement of her fingers to call him closer. He immediately moved to her and looked at her with tears in his eyes. He held her palm tightly and planted many kisses on it. Her palm was completely drenched in Sunny's tears and she gestured to him not to cry.

"Why did you do that, Mom?" he asked, crying. She smiled in a restrained way.

"Neha," she murmured. "Call her!" she muttered slowly. He ran to her. Neha ran inside with her mother.

"Neha... Come close to me, beta," she muttered, trying to speak. Neha went close to her, and Rekha gestured at them to hold their hands together; but they did not. She beckoned Neha's mother closer.

Neha's mother bent towards her, expressing her gratitude. "We can't repay you in this lifetime for what you have done for us. You are like god! You saved all of us, behenji!"

"You can, you can pay!" she muttered. Neha's mother gave her a surprised look. She made Sunny and Neha hold hands and told Neha's mother, "You can pay by giving your daughter to me for a lifetime. I am asking for your daughter's hand in marriage for my son, forever. I wish to see her as my daughter-in-law. I will be obliged if you can do me that favour," she muttered with a smile. Neha's mother was overwhelmed. Sunny's mother released her tension. A few days ago, she was crying and wondering who would take care of her daughter after her father. Now, she was given a perfect family for her daughter, and her husband got a new life as well. She was touched by this big move that Sunny's mom had taken for her family. Sunny and Neha embraced her for the irreparable sacrifice that she had made to bring happiness into her son's life.

"Mom, once again you have put your own life at stake for me! I would never have forgiven myself if something had happened to you." Sunny sobbed, pressing his face against her palm.

"I knew it, beta, that she has become your life!" she replied, caressing his hair and with her motherly touch. Once again, *she gave him life.*

Epilogue

"Hello sweetheart!"

"Oh! Hi Golu."

"Where were you the whole day? You did not answer my calls in afternoon?" Sunny said.

"I am so sooooo happy. I am too excited about our wedding day. You know what! I bought matching jewellery for my wedding lehenga today. I also visited the Lakme salon to check the range of bridal make-up they offer. You know what they said? They have a new make-up voucher to be launched this month and I will be the first bride to be benefited by it. It is all so exciting, Sunny. I am so lucky. I was busy all day, hopping from one shop to another. That is why I could not answer your call in the afternoon. Was it anything urgent?" Neha said all that in one go, indicating her excitement about the wedding preparations.

"That's so good! Neha, finally all your dreams are turning real. You will go to a decent college and do your MBA, marry according to your choice…great going girl! Your Shiv ji is very kind to you, I must say. Anyway, there is one more tick in your wish list and I am dying to share it with you. Finally, the hotel staff vendor called Papa today to say that his calendar is free for

February 14th. And jaan, Papa has booked that rotating stage for us. Something that you always dreamt of. Standing on it, you wanted to garland me on our wedding day, remember?" Sunny's news made her happier, and moistened her eyes with happiness.

"God has completed the cycle, jaan. We are getting married on the same day we once parted on."

"Hey! I wanted to share this happy news with Neha. Sunny beta, you gave all the credit to your Dad. That's so bad beta, huhh," Mom said, checking her to-do list and raising her head to offer Sunny a cheerful smile.

"No Mom, I was just..." Sunny stammered.

He was cut short by his mother. "Just kidding, beta! You continue, after all, she is your would-be-wife," she said, blowing a kiss in the air.

He nodded with a smile and gestured a thumbs-up.

"Hey! Neha...."

"I got it Sunny. Needless to say, she is a marvellous lady, my sweet would-be-mother," she said and her voice turned emotional. "Sunny, we need to take special care of her and bestow her with all the love that she deserves. I promise you, I will never let her be sad in my lifetime," she added.

"I know, Neha. You both are my world. The 2 SHEs of my life – one gave me life, other became my life."

"Wow! Writer saab, nice line." They both laughed and continued their chatter.

Recommended Reading

Be My Perfect Ending

Arpit Vageria

Armaan and Sara meet in filmy style and quite obviously then, cannot help but fall in love. The passionate new romance in his life throws everything else aside, but little does he know that there's a storm headed their way.

Be My Perfect Ending is a story of love that knows no bounds, of endings that are far from ordinary, and new beginnings that hold a promise of LOVE.

Arpit Vageria writes scripts for Indian television for a living, and writes romance stories for the love of it. He is the bestselling author of *You Are My Reason to Smile, I Still Think About You* and *Chocolate Sauce*.

ISBN: 9789387022089; Pages: 200; MRP: INR 175/-; Binding: Paperback

---

Lost in Love

Arvind Parashar

Neil and Gauri find love in each other in the most unexpected way. He has just had a heartbreak, and she has always had a crush on him. Once together, life looks beautiful.

But not for long, as their world comes crashing with a tragic, life-turning event. This is a heart-wrenching romance thriller that is bound to move you and hit your soul as you take a plunge and get ***Lost in Love.***

Arvind Parashar is the bestselling author of *Messed Up! But All for Love*, and a well-known motivational speaker.

ISBN: 9789387022119; Pages: 176; MRP: INR 175/-; Binding: Paperback

Imperfect Misfits

Devanshi Sharma

Just like a scoop of vanilla ice cream makes the sizzling chocolate brownie delicious, these best friends complimented each other. A chef by passion, Tiasha jumps and waves through her professional choices, while Aakaash, the witty stand-up comedian, knows exactly what he wants.

It gets complicated when love tries to sneak in. Will their friendship survive on this journey of love?

Imperfect Misfits is a story of perfect misfits, food, frolic, emotions and their endless imperfections.

Devanshi Sharma is a young and dynamic author with three books to her credit, the latest being the hot-selling *No Matter What I Do.*

ISBN: 9789387022072; Pages: 208; MRP: INR 175/-; Binding: Paperback

---

My Mute Girlfriend

Himanshu Rai

Rohan is a telecom professional posted in Meerut and misses his girlfriend from college days, who had stopped interacting with him, without giving any reason. Although she had always stood by his side and her eyes reflected immense love, but she remained his mute girlfriend.

My Mute Girlfriend is a true romance story of how Rohan unravels the answers to why Vaidehi was mute for so long and how their life is about to change.

Himanshu is a telecom professional and storytelling has been his hobby. This is his third novel, reminiscing his college days.

ISBN: 9789387022140; Pages: 216; MRP: INR 195/-; Binding: Paperback

The Girl I Love

Amit Nangia

Myra loves Kairav and she does not even remember since when! Not just his best friend, she is also his partner in a successful dream start-up. Kairav cannot seem to see her more than a best friend, but turns to her every time he needs love and support.

Can Myra break out of her going-nowhere relationship with Kairav? Will Kairav ever figure out a relationship beyond his no-commitment status, to discover the girl he loves?

Amit Nangia creates brand advertisements by the day and writes romance novels by the night. He has worked on creating award-winning advertising campaigns like *Har ek friend zaroori hota hai* and many more.

ISBN: 9789387022164; Pages: 176; MRP: INR 175/-; Binding: Paperback

---

The One from the Stars

Keshav Aneel

Vishesh is a dreamer, and cannot see himself settling in a 9 to 5 job. His loved ones leave his side when, he is diagnosed with severe OCD.

Will a dreamer be sacrificed for social standing? Will a heart be crushed to uphold a hollow image?

This is Vishesh's intense story of repeatedly falling down and trying to get up on his own, to prove that everyone who dares to follow their heart is special.

Keshav is a lyricist and works as a motivational speaker with his prime focus on helping people follow their inner calling. He has also authored the bestselling book *Promise Me a Million Times.*

ISBN: 9789380349725; Pages: 168; MRP: INR 175/-; Binding: Paperback

Love A Little Stronger

Preeti Shenoy

Life is a collection of moments, some memorable and some mundane. Often it is the tiniest things that bring the greatest joy, even though at that time, we have no idea that what we are witnessing may be magical, something that we will talk about and laugh over after many years.

Packed with her hilarious narratives, poignant observations and a writing style loved by millions across the world, this book is certain to strike a chord with anybody who has children or who has been a child, themselves!

For those who have read *34 Bubblegums* and *Candies*, this is a new version, with many additional stories. For others, it is a heart-warming, hilarious, and inspiring collection of true anecdotes from the author's life, telling us to *Love A Little Stronger*, no matter what happens.

Preeti Shenoy is the bestselling author of *Life is What You Make It* and nine other titles. Her books have been translated into several Indian and foreign languages. She is among the highest selling authors in India. She is also a speaker, columnist, and artist. Preeti has been featured on *BBC, Conde Nast, Verve, India Today* and all other major media.

ISBN: 9789387022133; Pages: 176; MRP: INR 175/-; Binding: Paperback

Upcoming title by the same author

Till My Heart Beats

I will be there for you

She was treading with heavy steps, but not as heavy as her heart. She had to endure excruciating pain to make those movements. She was struggling to balance; falling down and standing up multiple times, till she collapsed on her knees. She jolted up and walked hastily, making brisk movements, unfazed of the blood oozing out of her bruises and the hanging torn pieces of her clothes. She reached the corner of that road, and raised her hand to see the blood-stained knife. She enigmatically gazed at it for a few seconds and slowly moved it towards her neck.

"I love you, honey, and will always do… even after I die. Please don't misunderstand me. I have to do this because I can't see you in pain. You have done a lot for me… I am treasuring all those memories and taking them with my soul. Maybe this is what is written in our destiny… maybe we will meet in our next birth… The only regret is I couldn't give you the love you deserve… I couldn't walk along with you till the end…" Her speech stuttered and dragged through her quivering dried lips and a tear marked its way wetting them. Her thoughts rolled down the memory lane to recall the song he used to sing for her.

Whether it's the darkness or light,
Whether it's pain or delight;
Whether it's a thorny road
Or a smooth ride;
Whether it's close or far away,
Where the horizon meets,
I will be there for you
Till my heart beats…